SAFETY

FIRST

YOU'RE not paid to take risks

SAFETY FIRST

VINTAGE POSTERS FROM RoSPA's ARCHIVE

Paul Rennie

with a foreword by
Lord McKenzie of Luton

Saraband

Published by Saraband
Suite 202, 98 Woodlands Road
Glasgow, G3 6HB, Scotland
www.saraband.net

Text by Paul Rennie
Editor: Craig Hillsley

Previous pages: A poster by Leonard Cusden illustrating the risk of fire caused by cigarettes; a 1961 poster by Leonard Woy urging caution against taking unnecessary risks in the workplace.

ISBN: 9781908643728

Printed in the European Union on paper from sustainable sources.

CONTENTS

FOREWORD

The Royal Society for the Prevention of Accidents (RoSPA) believes that everyone has the right to enjoy a more fulfilling life by understanding how to identify and manage risk.

This belief has been at the heart of RoSPA's approach to accident prevention since the charity's inception in the early years of the twentieth century and, put into practice, it results in fewer people being killed or seriously hurt in accidents – and more people possessing the skills and the knowledge they need to make the most of their lives.

Various methods of bringing accident prevention to people, whether they're at work, at home or at play, have been employed by RoSPA during its long history, and this important and attractive book documents what we now look back on as a 'golden age' of public information, when a range of essential messages disseminated from a few trusted sources were embraced by a nation of people – many of whom had experienced serious injury and death caused in the violence of war.

Throughout much of the twentieth century, these messages – often communicated by RoSPA, as this book testifies, through leading-edge poster art – formed a critical part of a consensus to prevent unnecessary harm, through education, engineering and enforcement. This approach paid dividends as, during the course of the last century, the number of accidental deaths and life-changing injuries has fallen dramatically in our workplaces and on our roads.

Since then, much has changed – but much still stays the same.

Accidents currently kill about 14,000 people every year, and injure millions more. They continue to be the top cause of early preventable death for most of our lives, and are responsible for about a third of the twenty million attendances at Accident & Emergency units in the UK every year. Of even more serious concern today is the rising number of people who are being killed or injured in the home or during leisure activities.

But even in this information-saturated age of social media and 24-hour news, there is much that these now 'vintage' posters can tell us about the power of prevention: that a little effort, a little forward planning – and above all, a little knowledge, can make a big difference in our quest to get the balance right between carelessness on the one hand, and risk-aversion on the other. Neither is a desirable trait in a mature and modern society.

It is fitting that as our charity celebrates its centenary, the rediscovery of these posters should stand at the intersection of a proud past and a promising future – promising, because RoSPA stands ready to serve the nation again, by providing our families, our colleagues and our friends, with all of the skills and confidence they need to lead more fulfilling lives – free of the fear of accidental injury.

Lord McKenzie of Luton
President, The Royal Society for the Prevention of Accidents

INTRODUCTION

The Royal Society for the Prevention of Accidents (RoSPA) is an independent charity that, for one hundred years, has promoted safety awareness in the UK and around the world – and it has done so with phenomenal success. Many of the posters and slogans used in the society's campaigns have imprinted themselves on our national consciousness, changing our behaviours and, by extension, making us safer.

Traditionally, RoSPA's campaigns focused on occupational, road and home safety, and that is still the case today, though it now also directs resources to education and leisure safety. For nearly all of its history, the society has made imaginative use of poster art, design and illustration to communicate its messages effectively.

This book, which celebrates a century of safety campaigning, is the first to present the history of RoSPA by reference to its poster archive. It highlights some of the major designers who participated in RoSPA's campaigns, before going on to consider the technical aspects of the design and printing of the RoSPA posters. In the late 1990s, when I first began to investigate the history of safety posters, they seemed to have disappeared. This was, in part, a reflection of the shift across much of Britain towards a post-industrial economy. As the economy changed, so the messages migrated to other channels – radio, television, the nascent Internet – where they would have the most impact in the modern world.

When I contacted RoSPA to ask about their historical poster campaigns, I was told that the archive had been lost. Lost, in the gaps between its various moves and organisational restructurings.

But the archive was not so much lost, it turns out, as stored. Hundreds of posters, designs and pieces of artwork were rediscovered by accident during 2011, as a consequence of the sale and clearing of an old warehouse. Many of those superb images are reproduced in this book.

From the first, RoSPA's efforts were largely promoted through 'visual communication' – the use of skills such as design, drawing, illustration and typography in order to educate an audience. The extensive use of visual

"All the same they should have been good for another 500 miles at least"

HOW ARE YOUR BRAKES —— & TYRES ?

Issued by the National Safety First Association
Terminal House, 52 Grosvenor Gardens, London, S.W.1

A visual language developed through RoSPA's safety posters, which were created by the best graphic designers and illustrators – including Fougasse (left, also well known for his war poster campaigns 'Careless Talk Costs Lives' and for his London Transport posters), and Eckersley (opposite). Both made use of bold designs and simple shapes.

communication aligned RoSPA with a group of organisations that, by virtue of the scale and reach of their efforts, were at the very forefront of communication design in Britain. The leading-edge posters of London Transport, Shell-Mex and BP Ltd, the General Post Office, the Empire Marketing Board, and the large railway companies, are already well known; the RoSPA posters should be ranked alongside these pioneers and deserve to be more widely known.

However, the complete RoSPA story, told here, extends far beyond the posters and original objectives of the society's founders (to improve pedestrian awareness of new-fangled motor vehicles). It also includes Ministers of State, the design establishment and émigré designers. It is a story that has seen such a successful transformation in working conditions that, even on very large construction and civil-engineering projects, fatalities are nowadays very rare. The creation of increasingly safe environments for work, rest and play has been one of the great achievements of twentieth-century Britain. RoSPA's centenary should give everyone just cause for celebration.

Safety, Visual Communication and Modern Britain

The concept of safety is quite straightforward. At a basic level we understand it as safety from predatory violence. Now, thankfully and for the most part, we live beyond this red-in-tooth-and-claw-survival-of-the-fittest arrangement. Nevertheless, the continuing acceleration of modern society and the ferociousness of the mechanised world provide ample reason for safety issues to remain important.

The present-day mechanised world has evolved from the industrialisation of the

eighteenth century. At first, the 'theatre of machines' was confined to factories and workshops, but it expanded to a national scale during the nineteenth century with the development of the railway network. As the world became increasingly mechanised, so it became faster, more integrated, more automated – more overwhelming! Nowadays, of course, technology extends into every part of our lives and reaches across national boundaries.

Above: The Tufty Club was formed in 1961 and became an immediate hit with children. Opposite: Common sense precautions in the workplace.
Overleaf: Iconic road safety posters for motorcyclists, by Roland Davies. Following pages: A selection of RoSPA's poster output covering various campaigns.

The rapid acceleration of life had significant social and political consequence too; as people and things sped up, they changed relative position. In the twentieth and twenty-first centuries the continuous and uninterrupted working of the mechanised world has become a symbol of political, administrative and social stability. The promotion of safety has, in consequence, also become an expression of a consistent and stable social environment. The posters in this book are not just safety propaganda and graphic design; they are also visual expressions of the systemic relations between man and machine.

Some of Britain's biggest industries have, in the past, been so dangerous that they were obliged to provide orphanages for the destitute children of deceased workers. The big railway companies, the merchant marine and even the Royal Mail were required, at various times, to accept this tragic and terrible responsibility.

The concept of modern safety, which RoSPA addresses, emerged during 1916 as a consequence of machine war and the danger it posed to the civilian population. Britain's manufacturing industry now had military objectives, which produced a large increase in the volume of traffic and, because of mechanisation, there was also a substantial increase in the speed of that traffic. The subsequent rise in road accidents was understood as both an individual trauma and a blow to the war economy. After the armistice, the scope of the society's efforts quickly expanded to address issues of industrial safety and home safety.

In these circumstances, accident prevention became not simply a question of personal responsibility; it also became a matter of public health, policy and economics.

accidents
don't just happen
**they are
CAUSED**

Above and opposite: RoSPA has always urged its
members to identify risk and to act accordingly.

The acceleration of life that gave rise to the
origins of RoSPA is a characteristic of the
international cultural phenomenon known as
modernism, which we generally describe as
an appeal to new ideas, images and materials.
Modernism embraces scientific reason and
economic rationalism in order to ensure the
successful, progressive and continuous transformation of society.

During the twentieth century, modernism
was the major template for rebuilding after
both World Wars.

The immediate aftermath of World War I
was a period of great upheaval across Europe.
As well as the need to rebuild and transform
politics and the economy to a non-war footing,
massive social changes had taken place as a
result of the war. This provided the ideal starting point for modernist renewal and enhanced
social progress, often working in tandem.

The belief in social progress was given
expression through the extension of the democratic body and in a range of popular-front
policies. These ideas had to be communicated
and a variety of new mass media – radio broad-
casting, film, photography – began to shape
the beginnings of public relations in Britain.

This time saw the emergence of a new, contemporary form of print culture based on the
integration of image and text, and the organisation of information. This was the beginning
of graphic design.

In Britain, the Design and Industries
Association (DIA) promoted a comfortable
form of modernity that combined an arts-
and-crafts sensibility with an industrial logic
of production. At the same time, the large
organisations that emerged after World War I
chose to promote themselves through the production of advertising posters and other visual
material – unsurprisingly, given the success
of Britain's propaganda effort during the war.
During the 1920s and 1930s, the members of
the DIA transformed the use of public relations and posters, successfully conveying messages that went far beyond the literal expression of straightforward advertising.

The fact that RoSPA also used the new kinds
of posters to spread its messages suggests
this was an organisation that, from the first,
embraced modern forms of communication.
The accident prevention posters presented in
this book offer compelling evidence of a progressive engagement, through design, with
issues of public health in Britain.

ICE&SNOW mind how you go

LET'S HAVE A..

SAFETY
RECORD
TO CROW ABOUT

CHAPTER 1

RoSPA AND THE TWO WORLD WARS

1916–1945

The origins of RoSPA date back to the end of 1916, the midway point of World War I and a time when Britain was immersed in a state of 'total war', with forced conscription being introduced for the first time. As well as the massive military operation that was taking place on the Continent, the civilian population of Britain was also playing its part, with the country's economy and industry largely turned over to supporting the war effort.

New Dangers on the Roads

The mechanisation of the war led to a greatly increased number of road accidents, mainly due to the very large increase in the number of motor vehicles on the road. This was especially the case in the towns and cities attached to military garrisons, and to those urban areas involved in industrial war production. The increase of motor traffic, which of course moved at much greater speed than the horse-drawn vehicles people were used to, created a number of problems – which were made worse by the advent of air attack and the consequent blackout of street lighting. New rules of engagement between drivers and pedestrians were drawn up and new road design began to separate different kinds of road user.

The origins of RoSPA can be found in the London 'Safety First' Council (LSFC), which was formed to co-ordinate pedestrian awareness of the dangers associated with the increased volume and speed of motor traffic. From the first, the LSFC collected reports of accidents. This data allowed for all the organisation's proposals to be evidence-based, and aligned the LSFC with other progressive organisations using scientific methods.

The council's first meeting acknowledged the 'alarming increase' in accidents as justification for its efforts. Given the specific context of war, the council promoted the need for safer road sense as part of a patriotic war effort, thus appealing to the public's sense of duty. The council also established a safe driving competition for professional drivers employed within Greater London. This contest also acted as a means of identifying best practice.

Local activities on the ground were co-ordinated by a designated safety officer, drawn

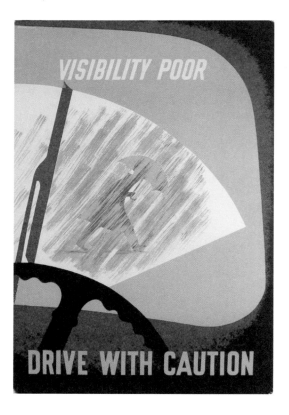

Left and opposite: From the first, issues of road safety have been a major concern for RoSPA, whether focused on road and weather conditions, pedestrian and driver awareness, driver courtesy, training, wearing seat belts, avoiding driving when tired, or driving under the influence of alcohol.

from the administrators of local government. In general, events such as talks and displays would take place during a specific week – what we would now call an 'awareness week' – making it easier to promote in the media.

The example of the LSFC was quickly followed by other cities where the mechanised war-economy and military activity made the urban environment more dangerous. The various campaigns were merged into a national organisation in 1923. This was called the National 'Safety First' Association (NSFA).

For most of the 1920s and 1930s, the NSFA remained primarily concerned with the promotion of road safety. The NSFA was instrumental in conceptualising a consistent set of motoring rules and integrating them into the Highway Code. The code was first published in 1931. The association also began to elaborate a series of badges and medals to distinguish the activities of its membership. This has continued, to the present, almost without interruption.

The advent of a coherent driver and vehicle licensing system, during 1930, also provided an opportunity for the association to publish *Many Happy Returns*. This small pamphlet was a humorous tract of advice for new drivers and was illustrated with line drawings by Cyril Kenneth Bird, the cartoonist also known as 'Fougasse' who's probably best known for his Careless Talk Costs Lives propaganda posters during World War II.

It is testimony to the NSFA's ambition and design-sense that they employed the likes of Bird, Hans Schleger (also known as 'Zero'), Edward McKnight Kauffer and Abram Games to promote their efforts before World War II. Each of these names is now acknowledged as amongst the most significant designers in Britain during the 1930s.

In addition to this relatively early engagement with design, the association also began, from the first, to engage its audiences through humour and wit. This was quite unusual, both in Britain and internationally. Traditionally, official communications have generally been expressed in a tone that reflected their serious-mindedness.

The use of humour in communication later became a staple of Britain's World War II experience. The general success of these efforts has contributed to the international reputation of the British sense of humour.

Opposite and above: Belisha beacons were introduced in 1934. Later, black-and-white striped road markings heralded the 'zebra crossing'. As with all safety measures, effective publicity was crucial.

Internationally, the promotion of safety awareness was much more limited before World War II. In America, safety issues were largely the individual responsibilities of the worker. Culturally, the US industrial worker was understood as a productive force. So, any accident immediately compromised this productive energy.

However, in Britain, safety awareness was considered to be everyone's concern, and its promotion was well organised. The NSFA established a series of regional safety committees, which reported to the National Executive. The National Executive, in turn, balanced objectives and resources within the national organisation through consultation with the finance and publicity committees.

The chief executive of the NSFA was Lt Colonel JAA Pickard, who had been recommended to the society through his interests in the field of road safety. During the 1930s, the principal activities of the association reflected the main interests of its executive and membership. But the coming of World War II transformed the balance of activities within the society through an alignment with the wider national interest.

Tackling Hazards in the Workplace

In 1918, the LSFC extended its activities through the creation of the British Industrial 'Safety First' Association (which was aligned with the NSFA in 1923). From the beginning, this organisation was national in scope. The specialist concern about workshop and factory safety focused efforts on the specific areas of manufacturing and production. The promotional material concerning industrial safety was made available, on a subscription basis, to member enterprises of the association.

The statutory framework for health and safety at work was established through a series of Factory Acts. These acts provided for a Factory Inspectorate, and established reporting standards in relation to fatalities within the workplace. The consistent reporting of accidents helped identify recurring patterns of tragedy within the workplace.

The Factories Act of 1937 established a discretionary duty-of-care towards workers. These issues were addressed by the NSFA through the production of simple single-colour posters for workshops.

The organisation's president from 1937 and during World War II was Lord Harry McGowan. Ironically, his business career had included the consolidation of the British explosives industry during World War I and the creation of the ICI industrial conglomerate. Perhaps because of the evident dangers associated with these industries, McGowan was an important, influential and tireless advocate of safety throughout. Lord McGowan famously declared that 'One of our fighters is missing, if you are off work with an accident.'

The role of president has been important in facing the legislature and guiding the process towards statutory regulation where necessary.

The organisation's design director at this time was HG Harry Winbolt. His role was to brief artists clearly and to encourage simple and dramatic designs that could be economically printed. Winbolt produced two important publications describing the significance of industrial safety. The first, published in the late 1930s, was *We Don't Want to Lose You So... We Think You Ought to Know*, with illustrations

Opposite page: From the 1930s, safety issues were considered everyone's concern – even Santa's!

by Philip Mendoza. Its title is a play on the words 'We don't want to lose you but we think you ought to go' from the popular World War I recruitment song, *Your King and Country Want You*. The second publication, produced in 1952, was *The Causes of Everyday Accidents in Factories*.

RoSPA and World War II

The events of World War II provide the crucial backdrop for understanding the more substantial role that the organisation (to be renamed RoSPA during the war years) would soon play in national life. The scale and significance of its activities developed due to the greater demands of the war effort.

Mr. Featherwate says...

'Correct handling
eases effort'

Within this context, the manufacture of military equipment was identified as a national priority, and every effort was made to increase efficiency and maintain production. Industrial accidents were quickly recognised as having a significant collective impact not only on production, but also on morale. Accordingly, health and safety at work was now a matter of urgency and employers were encouraged to adopt a duty-of-care to their workers by appeal to patriotic duty. This was especially the case in relation to the large number of new workers drafted into factories and workshops in an effort to boost production. The evident good sense of this arrangement was understood, within the context of war, as politically correct.

The early phase of the war immediately conspired to make these issues even more significant. The ill-fated British Expeditionary Force in France was obliged to retreat from Dunkirk during May and June of 1940. The successful evacuation of British troops from the beaches of northern France was recognised as an unlikely success. At the same time, the hasty retreat caused the British Army to lose nearly all of its heavy equipment. In consequence, the British war economy's productive effort was again increased.

The next phase of military action, after Dunkirk, saw German forces attempting to claim air superiority over Britain, prior to an invasion on the ground. The Battle of Britain, fought out over Kent and London during the summer of 1940, established that the RAF's Spitfires and Hurricanes were essential in order to maintain Britain's control of the air.

Left and opposite: Efficiency at work was recognised as a key contribution to the war effort.

DON'T FALL FOR THIS !

RIDE SAFELY

Good loading prevents transit damage

LEVEL OFF LOADS

STOW PACKAGES EVENLY

LIGHT & FRAGILE GOODS ON TOP

DON'T ACCEPT
packages unfit for transit

EXAMINE WAGONS
BEFORE LOADING

LOOK FOR
★ uneven floors ★
★ protruding bolts ★
★ defective roof & sides ★

Remove or cancel all
OLD LABELS
See that packages are
clearly & securely labelled

These pages: Bruce Angrave, a member of the Society of Industrial Artists, was influenced by the work of RoSPA's early illustrators.

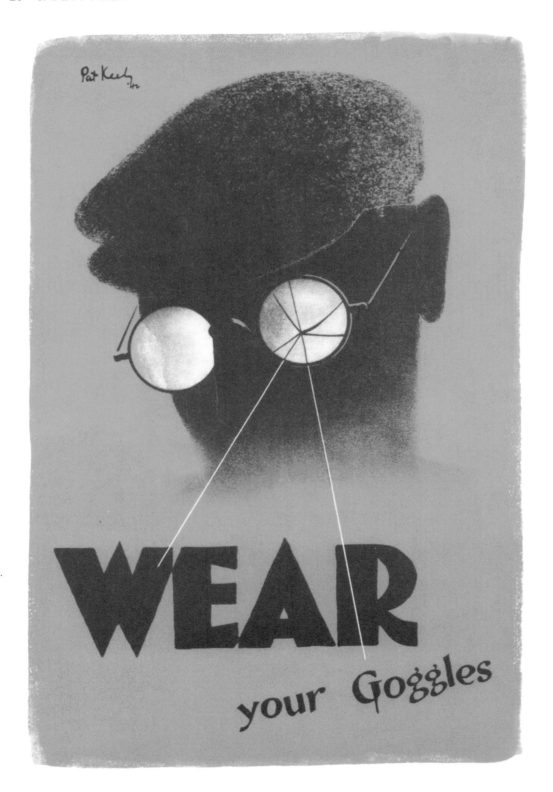

After the Battle of Britain, Germany launched a series of night bombing raids against the big cities and major industrial centres of Britain. The Blitz was an attempt to destroy Britain's civic and industrial infrastructure and, at the same time, to attack the civilian population and to undermine morale. Notwithstanding the terrible destruction associated with these raids, the Blitz was unsuccessful in its secondary objectives.

By the end of 1940, it was clear that 'Fortress Britain' would, all things remaining equal, be able to resist German aggression more or less indefinitely. Accordingly, plans could be made to extend the scope of war aims to include progressive social reform and post-war planning.

Against this background, the authorities noticed that hospital resources, made ready for the victims of enemy action were, in fact, being used to treat relatively minor industrial accidents and bumps from the blackout.

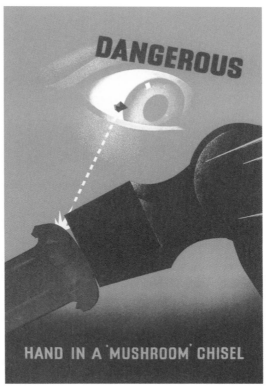

HAND IN A 'MUSHROOM' CHISEL

PROTECT your eyes

Workshop injuries were always personally debilitating and distressing. In addition, they were inconvenient for colleagues and, of course, impacted negatively upon the all-important production and efficiency of British industry.

Many workers suffered eye injuries as a result of flying debris, splinters and shards. These types of injury could very easily, and inexpensively, be reduced by appeal to the wearing of safety goggles. A series of posters addressing this specific issue became one of RoSPA's most famous campaigns.

These pages and overleaf: Eye and hand injuries were easily preventable industrial accidents. Through poster campaigns like these, RoSPA advocated the adoption of simple precautions including goggles and routine equipment checks.

TIME FOR REPAIR

BEFORE IT 'GETS' YOU THERE

RoSPA's thematic focus on eye, hand and foot injuries provided an unlikely pretext for surrealistic design during World War II. Surrealism had emerged in France and Belgium as a cultural reaction to World War I. André Breton, the founder of surrealism, appropriated the ideas of Sigmund Freud so as to conceptualise surrealism as providing a lively expression of the subconscious. In practical terms, this gave artists an opportunity to engage with a number of themes through association and transformation. These weren't entirely new techniques, but the appeal to the subconscious allowed for a wider range and variety of outcomes.

For the surrealists, the hand and the eye were parts of the body freighted with special significance. The heightened sensory sensitivity of

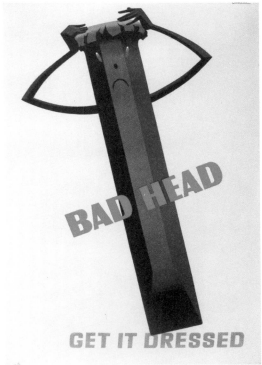

these organs gave them significance in relation to feeling and emotion. Accordingly, the surrealists were quick to explore the complex interaction of anxiety and desire afforded by these soft tissues.

A poster by Hans Schleger, the German émigré designer, showed a pedestrian figure with exaggerated eyes and ears. For Schleger, this implied that pedestrians should engage their senses, by using their eyes and ears, when crossing the road. At the same time, the pedestrian was, literally and surrealistically, transformed by this sensory focus.

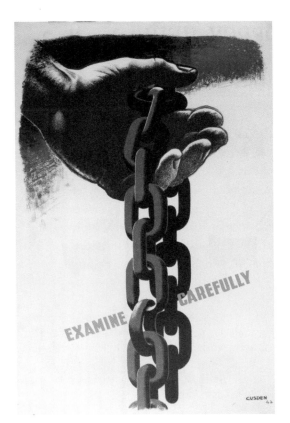

Opposite and above: The influence of surrealism on poster design can be seen in these posters, where visual and verbal puns are used.
Left: A more straightforward message, but nonetheless emphasising the hands.

DON'T TRY TO JUMP IT

USE A PIT PLANK

In visual terms, we can see this idea in the historical example of the homunculus. This is a figure whose physical appearance is determined by the physiology of feeling, so that parts of the body with high sensitivity are larger (and more highly developed) than less sensitive areas. For Schleger, the pedestrian was transformed, in the presence of road traffic, into a roadside homunculus.

In relation to industrial safety propaganda, hands and eyes became symbols to describe the dangers of the machine. These organs were also especially significant within the new, technical, sphere of production. Their obvious association to the positive qualities of precision and dexterity made them especially meaningful to workers. Accordingly, hand and eye were understood as defining a more nuanced relationship, for the worker, with the machine-tool and with productive efficiency.

The transformative potential of man and machine is well established in relation to science fiction. We are all familiar with the idea of the robot or cyborg. In the factory, the interface between man and machine is more complex. Historically, the machine had been understood, by workers at least, as a predatory monster. The description of time-and-motion as a form of efficiency provided for both a logic and tempo of production. It was entirely appropriate, in these circumstances, for artists to imagine the machine in transformative terms.

The problem of industrial safety could most generally be addressed through the promotion of safe working practices by establishing a consistent routine of activity. This was especially important given the effort demanded from a workforce largely new to factories and the production methods needed to supply the war machine.

We now know from cognitive psychology that all of our faculties, both mental and physical, develop through repeated use. So, routine and practice literally make perfect. And safe! Awareness campaigns were progressively orientated towards identifying and establishing routines or patterns of safety. Subsequently, a number of posters also addressed the issue of horseplay in factories and workshops.

Left and opposite: Establishing safe working routines – the subject of many posters like these, designed to illustrate the dangers inherent in tempting shortcuts.

Overleaf : Horseplay was a subject rich in inspiration for RoSPA's illustrators.

Royal Recognition for RoSPA

The greater significance of the safety message raised the organisation's profile, but also threatened its finances. The member firms could not, on their own, fund the greatly expanded requirement for safety posters and documentation.

In 1941 the organisation was granted royal patronage and was named the Royal Society for the Prevention of Accidents. This was a public acknowledgement of the importance of RoSPA and of its messages.

Accordingly, and for the duration of World War II, the concerns of accident prevention were aligned with those of the war effort: efficiency, morale and production. In these circumstances, the government chose to underwrite the publication of RoSPA's safety messages. This was achieved by attaching

'Horseplay' was associated with workers playing jokes, and the 'initiations' for young or new workers. The good-natured jokes were intended to establish the hierarchy of status across the factory floor, but in an environment of febrile effort and anxiety associated with war, these supposedly innocuous jokes often ended in minor injury.

Another theme of the campaigns was the prompt replacement of mushroomed tools – those tools damaged by repeated and long-term use. Eventually, metal shards or splinters may fly off and cause injury.

The advance of women into the industrial workforce also came to RoSPA's attention and some posters addressed women specifically. These posters typically concerned the correct attire for work: sensible shoes and practical hairstyles were suggested as best.

Bevin's experience in the British labour movement during the 1930s gave him a unique perspective on industrial relations. His vision of the war economy made the alignment between welfare and efficiency explicit. Bevin understood that welfare gains made during the war were unlikely to be immediately dismantled.

The appropriation of RoSPA's industrial service by the ministry, for the duration, may be understood as a strategic manoeuvre for better working conditions over the longer term.

Bevin had been introduced to Frank Pick, chief executive of London Transport, in the course of industrial arbitration between the representatives of the Central Area Bus Crews and their employers. An unlikely friendship between Bevin and Pick was formed as a consequence of these negotiations. The

RoSPA's industrial service to the Ministry of Labour and National Service. The minister in charge was Ernest Bevin, a trade union leader and Labour politician who had co-founded and served as the General Secretary of the powerful Transport and General Workers' Union from 1922 to 1940.

In 1940 Winston Churchill had formed an emergency and all-party coalition government to run the country during wartime. Churchill appointed Bevin as Minister of Labour and he succeeded in maximising the British labour supply, for both the armed services and domestic industrial production, and with a minimum of strikes and disruption.

Opposite, above and right: Countless posters were designed to warn of the dangers of mushroomed tools and the importance of using the best tool for the job.

mutual respect between these individuals, representing different sides of the argument, were augmented by their shared background within non-conformist religious communities. Indeed, the traditions of non-conformism extended, within RoSPA, to its printers, Loxley Brothers, of Sheffield, and to a number of its designers.

Pick would also have taken great pride in describing the integrated design of his organisation. Pick and his railway colleagues had pioneered scientific management, which involved collecting data and making decisions based on verifiable records. The reporting standards for accidents and injuries, collected by RoSPA, provided the same basis for evidence-based and progressive reform of the workplace.

The personalities and expertise of McGowan, Bevin and Pick allowed for the strategic alignment of national, industrial and worker interests behind RoSPA's safety movement.

The demands of industrial production during World War II were such that RoSPA's industrial service, with its association with the Ministry of Labour, became the largest and most extensive of its services. At the height of this effort, some half a million posters were displayed in factories and workshops around Britain.

A combination of graphic posters, illustrational posters and slogan posters were supplied to workshops and factories. Thus, a relatively small selection of posters could be displayed in new combinations and the presentation kept fresh. The posters were supplemented by a series of notes, strip-cartoons and educational material for discussion. In addition to all this, factory managers were obliged to provide permanent display areas for poster materials and a dedicated space for safety training.

The training documents featuring cartoons and humour were built around the hapless, but enthusiastic, figure of Percy Vere, created by Philip Mendoza. The comic drawings were matched with memorable humorous verses and published in coloured pamphlet form. These pamphlets, called *Percy Verses*, were published in large editions and made available over a period of years.

This all provided for a much more consistent delivery of safety messages in factories. The displays also integrated safety organisation into the life, routine and fabric of the workplace.

An Epic Wartime Poster Campaign

As the rapid expansion of the war economy required a much-increased output of RoSPA's material, the Ministry of Labour ensured that the necessary funding was available. The ambitions of RoSPA were to publish, every year, about one hundred new posters, double crown (30" x 20") or smaller. These would be printed in increasingly large editions to serve the growing membership.

In order to manage this increased level of activity, it was decided that poster designs should be chosen by panel. The publicity committee, based in London, oversaw the effectiveness of RoSPA's propaganda output. Their terms of reference were to guide and control publicity within the financial constraints specified by the management and finance committees. In addition, they were to control the society's exhibition policy, to advise on film policy, to review the work of RoSPA's operations division and to report to the executive on all of the above. The committee was also encouraged to adopt a critical position in relation to poster design.

The panel was initially made up of a RoSPA representative, a Mr T Goodall, and various external experts, including Fleetwood Pritchard (Honorary Adviser to the Ministry of War Transport), and Mary Field, who was responsible for film-making activities. The committee chose posters from open submissions. This process, ad hoc at best, was regularised by the addition to the panel, during 1941, of Ashley Havinden.

Above: Leonard Cusden was one of RoSPA's key poster artists. Opposite: Many of RoSPA's most effective and attractive graphic designs produced during World War II were illustrated by Salford-born Tom Eckersley. During his long and prolific career, he worked for the RAF and London Transport as well as producing safety posters like these for RoSPA.

Havinden was a successful and experienced advertising executive and had helped establish the Crawford agency's Berlin office during the 1920s. He had therefore been exposed to the progressive design ideas of the Bauhaus and understood the new design to be both effective and economical. Under Havinden's guidance, the panel gathered together a standing roster of experienced commercial artists and designers who could be called upon to design posters at regular intervals. The panel was further strengthened by the addition of Francis Meynell, publisher.

Meynell was one of the most considerable figures in the revival of printing that occurred in Britain between the wars. Together with Oliver Simon and Stanley Morison he was responsible for extending an arts-and-crafts aesthetic sensibility beyond the private press movement and into the mainstream of commercial printing.

Meynell promoted careful printing with machine setting so as to produce new standards of quality in mass-market printing. His commitment to machine printing was based on economy and a belief that craft-tradition and machine printing were not incompatible.

The presence of both Havinden and Meynell on the RoSPA publicity committee effectively illustrates the society's commitment to good design and effective communications.

The publicity committee also took an interest in the effective display of their material. It was quickly realised that each workplace should try to create a more or less permanent state of display material. This involved the creation of display environments within the works where a changing series of posters could be displayed. It was felt important that

specific sites should be created so that their maintenance could be effectively monitored. Also, it was felt that such displays, by virtue of their being thought through and co-ordinated, would be more effective than an ad hoc display of material wherever space allowed. Thus was the publicity material cemented into the fabric of industrial buildings.

Havinden recalled that, from the 1920s onwards, he had been impressed by 'the dynamic potential of graphic communication to project effectively'. This was especially true where the prevailing context was one of static

Above and opposite: The poster committee drove up standards of both design and production by encouraging the use of the best available artists and ensuring that printing was quality controlled.

FENCE ALL OPENINGS

society's accounts also included the names of Hans Schleger, HA Rothholz, Manfred Reiss, and those also of Polish émigrés, Jan Lewitt and George Him. All of these designers had established themselves in Europe and would have been known to Havinden from his days in Berlin, and at Crawford's office in London. The creative talent chosen by Havinden, and used by RoSPA, should be recognised as an explicit association with European modernism in graphic design.

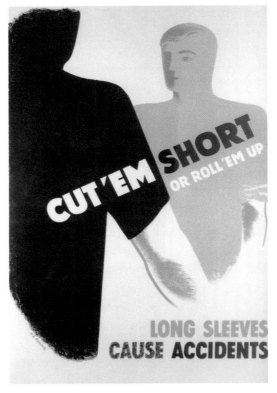

CUT 'EM SHORT OR ROLL 'EM UP

LONG SLEEVES CAUSE ACCIDENTS

and uninspired communication. The factory context of RoSPA's official communications allowed for just such development.

RoSPA's financial accounts recorded payments to designers and artists and it is therefore possible to establish a list of the artists used and the frequency with which they were employed. Among the first names that appeared, in 1939, was that of Abram Games. Later, those of Tom Eckersley and Eric Lombers appeared. Havinden's contacts within the commercial art environment and his interest in progressive design gave him the chance to use artists and designers overlooked by the more mainstream creative directors of the Ministry of Information. The roll call of designers listed and credited in the

Above and opposite: HA Rothholz (above) and Manfred Reiss were amongst the artists employed regularly by RoSPA's poster committee. Their modernist graphic style is exemplified in factors including the use of abstraction.

KEEP GUARD

BETWEEN YOU & DANGER

avant-garde in design, as the most dynamic and energetic of shapes. Accordingly, the triangular warning-sign shape used across RoSPA's various graphic identities became explicitly associated with modern design thinking.

The efforts of Havinden in securing a foothold for modern design in RoSPA's activities is evidence that, whatever the difficulties of the wartime environment, Britain could embrace new ideas. But stylistic experimentation in graphic design would have counted for nothing if it had not also been both economical and effective.

The economics of visual communications, founded on the use of the most up-to-date printing technology and the ruthless simplifications of the design brief, allowed RoSPA to circulate ever-increasing numbers of posters within the industrial community. This activity was continued after the war and until the 1990s as a major part of RoSPA's work.

Notwithstanding the transformations of British industry, the RoSPA posters from World War II and the immediate post-war period can be identified as significant elements within the technocratic development of both industrial management and of the management of a nascent creative economy.

Lord McGowan, RoSPA's president at the time, noted that the industrial safety campaigns of the war years 'achieved successive reductions in the accident rate'.

It's interesting to note that avant-garde experiments in graphic communication had, from the 1920s, established a visual language derived entirely from colour and form. The experiments of El Lissitsky, in Germany and the USSR, had suggested that circles, squares and triangles could be arranged meaningfully. The triangle was recognised, amongst the

Left and opposite: These posters illustrated several aspects of the visual language developed by RoSPA's poster committee. The triangle, shown opposite, became an instantly recognisable symbol of warning. Hands could signify gestures, labour or simply human agency. Simplicity was often the key.

COURTESY
is infectious

CHAPTER 2

RoSPA IN POST-WAR BRITAIN

After the war, RoSPA began to re-orientate itself to the changing patterns of civilian life. The increasingly fast pace of the modern world, advancing technology, widespread prosperity and new leisure opportunities associated with the post-war boom brought a new range of dangers.

Road Safety

After World War II, the great expansion of car ownership was not only about the number of vehicles on the road, it was also about the profile of the typical driver. Car ownership became much more widely spread across the entire population. In consequence, the expression and tone of the messages associated with driving advice needed to change.

In the immediate aftermath of the war, RoSPA began to promote the idea of road courtesy, especially between drivers and pedestrians, as a way of managing more congested driving environments. This idea was a natural development of the driving advice provided by Cyril Kenneth Bird in his pre-war illustrated pamphlet, *You Have Been Warned – A Complete Guide to the Road*.

With hindsight, the appeal to manners seems overly optimistic. Nevertheless, and in the absence of statutory regulation, it was a sensible place to start. Over the next few years,

Left, above, opposite and overleaf: RoSPA had to convey the message through its posters that road safety was a matter for pedestrians, drivers and cyclists alike; all road users had to be addressed.

NATIONAL "SAFE DRIVING" COMPETITION

THE PURPOSE OF THE COMPETITION

To build up an army of reliable, alert, resourceful and courteous drivers whose aim is complete freedom from accident.

THE CONDITIONS AND AWARDS

The Competition is open to all paid drivers who must be entered by their employers.

A Diploma is given to every driver who has no blameworthy accident and is free from conviction for certain specified offences each year; after five consecutive years of blameless driving a medal is given, and after ten years a further medal with higher awards for longer periods.

A WORD TO EMPLOYERS

The Competition is a means of making a positive contribution towards greater road safety.

Accident-free drivers save you expense and inconvenience. A reputation for reliability is established.

WHAT THE DRIVER CAN GAIN

A reputation for courtesy and comradeship on the road.

The satisfaction of setting a good example to all road users.

A valuable testimonial in the event of change of employment.

Enter Now!

FOR FURTHER INFORMATION APPLY TO:-

Your Local Authority

or

The Royal Society for the Prevention of Accidents

Terminal House, 52 Grosvenor Gardens, London, S.W. I.

RoSPA's reporting revealed the extent of injury associated with road traffic and prepared the ground for a number of important campaigns.

These campaigns were aimed at highlighting the tragic consequences of a number of issues: the consequences of drinking alcohol and driving, of not wearing a seat belt and, for motorcyclists, of not wearing a crash helmet.

The drink-driving campaign was based on the empirical evidence gathered by RoSPA. The Christmas period festivities consistently revealed an unhappy spike in the numbers of people killed or injured on the road. As the social acceptability of drinking and driving was deeply ingrained, the campaign against it has required continuous repetition over the years in order to achieve success.

There was also a long-running campaign to persuade drivers of the need to wear a seat

belt. The evident success of this campaign suggested that passengers and children in the rear of the car could also benefit from the wearing of seat belts.

The wearing of crash helmets was promoted to address the very serious types of injury associated with motorcycle accidents. However, the idea of motorcycling has always combined freedom and excitement for its enthusiasts, so this campaign also required careful persuasion and convincing argument.

Left, above and opposite: Drink-driving often receives extra media attention during the festive season, but RoSPA campaigns vigorously year-round against drinking and driving. Campaigns include raising awareness of the 'morning after' residual effects of alcohol on safe driving.

MAKE SURE THEY'RE SAFE

ROAD SAFETY DEPENDS ON YOU

In 1973, crash helmets became obligatory for motorcyclists.

The wearing of seat belts by drivers and passengers, advocated since the 1960s, only became law in 1981. This marked the end of a long process, including several frustrated attempts at legislation.

The timeline of progress outlined in the appendix (page 149) shows the significance of RoSPA's parliamentary representation and of the tenacity required to achieve success.

The period after the introduction of this legislation saw a reduction in road fatalities and serious injuries. However, the seat belt, drink-driving and safety helmet campaigns were each contested at every step of the long journey into statute. In practical terms, these campaigns' ultimate success required both

Each of these issues was eventually consolidated into the statutory regulation of road traffic – though only after a concerted and prolonged effort of campaigning and negotiation. The representation of RoSPA, within the legislature and in the person of the society's president, helped guide this process to its successful conclusion.

The criminality of drink-driving was formally recognised in 1965. Fifty years of continuous reminding later, drink-driving is now much less prevalent, although the campaign continues for a lower limit across the whole of the UK.

Above and right: RoSPA campaigned long and hard for compulsory crash helmets for motorcyclists and mandatory usage of seat belts in cars. Opposite and overleaf: Posters highlighting the need for extra care in bad weather conditions.

IT'S A GREAT LIFE

Don't throw it away
– keep to the highway code

RoSPA

the continuous repetition of simple messages and a long-term engagement with the administrative processes of the legislature.

The presidents of RoSPA have been the traditional interface with the legislature. A full list of RoSPA presidents throughout the last one hundred years can be found in the appendices (page 150).

Pedestrian Safety – The Tufty Club and the Green Cross Code

For many people in Britain, the idea of road safety began with RoSPA's pedestrian training in the form of the Tufty Club. The Cycling Proficiency test was another rite of passage that defined a sense of mobility and freedom for many young people.

Below: The Cycling Proficiency test was launched in 1947, and (opposite) cycle safety has remained one of RoSPA's most important campaign subjects, whether aimed at cyclists or motorists.

One of RoSPA's principal activities was, from the first, teaching young children how to engage safely with road traffic. Tufty Fluffytail, the squirrel, was created in 1953 by Elsie Mills MBE. Tufty became the protagonist of a series of stories that were designed to promote safety through the consistent repetition of a simple routine of practical steps.

The use of animals has long been a standard way of engaging the interest of young children in books and stories. Tufty was entirely appropriate and comprehensible as a means of providing a consistent framework for safety education around the UK. RoSPA encouraged the formation of local safety groups in affiliation through the Tufty Club. The club was formed in 1961 and, by 1962, it had 60,000 young children as members. By 1966, there were 2,000 different groups affiliated to the scheme. At its height in the early 1970s, the scheme had 24,000 groups affiliated throughout the UK. Tufty's popularity continued well into the 1980s.

The interaction of motor traffic and pedestrians was, as a response to increased traffic levels, more carefully managed. The late 1960s saw the introduction of dedicated pedestrian bridges and tunnels as part of road-building schemes.

The pedestrian crossing was also modernised. The addition of sequential lights effectively controlled the interaction between people and traffic.

Don't be trapped by turning traffic

Good maintenance
and sound brakes matter!

always close the garden gate

play in a safe place

Do you know the Green Cross code?

stop at the ker

always close the garden gate

play in a safe place

Do you know the Green Cross code?

KERB DRILL

1. AT THE KERB STOP
2. LOOK RIGHT
3. LOOK LEFT
4. LOOK RIGHT AGAIN
5. THEN IF ALL CLEAR —
   WALK STRAIGHT ACROSS

Greetings from Tufty

The School Patrol sees Tufty and his friends across the road in safety

STOP CHILDREN

Best Wishes

One of RoSPA's principal goals is to promote safety for young children – including inculcating safer behaviour near roads. Illustrated on this spread are scenes involving Tufty Fluffytail and his friends, whilst other Kerb Drill messages are shown overleaf.

March across
when the road is clear

Always do your kerb drill

Previous generations of children were generally afforded more freedom to play outside, unsupervised by adults – which meant that it was important to teach responsibility at an early age. Older children were often tasked with looking after their younger siblings. Many of RoSPA's posters were designed to appeal directly to children to reinforce basic safety messages across all age groups.

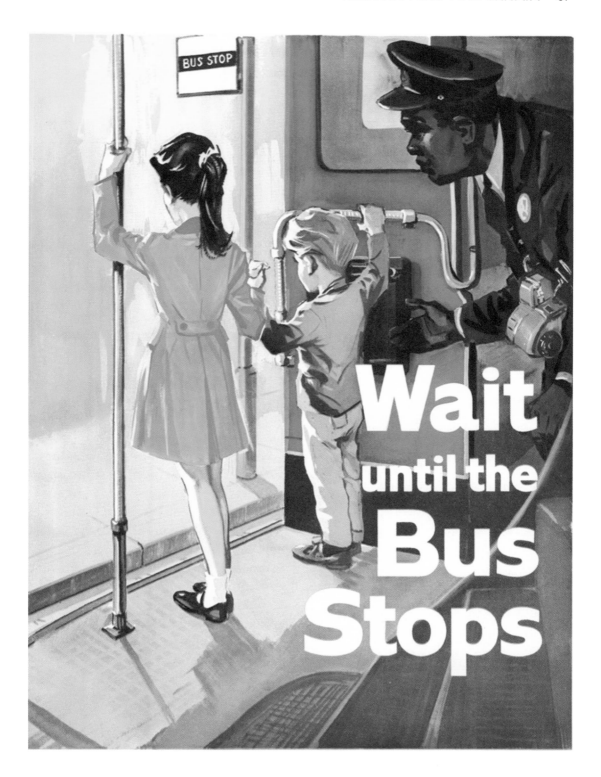

The Green Cross code ✗

THE CODE

First find a safe place to cross, then stop.

Stand on the pavement near the kerb.

Look all round for traffic and listen.

If traffic is coming, let it pass. Look all round again.

When there is no traffic near walk straight across the road.

Keep looking and listening for traffic while you cross.

THE SAFEST PLACES TO CROSS ARE

Pedestrian crossings

Subways

Foot bridges

Traffic lights

Where there are islands in the middle of the road

Where a policeman, school crossing patrol or a traffic warden is stopping traffic

OTHER SAFE PLACES ARE

Away from parked cars

Away from bends

Away from road junctions

With all these changes taking place, a new tone of instructions was required and, in 1970, the Department for Transport introduced the Green Cross Code.

The new code aimed to help people cross the road safely, and although it has changed somewhat over the years, the Green Cross Code of today is still recognisably similar to that of 1970, which encouraged us to 'Think, Stop, Use your Eyes and Ears'.

The associated education programme also sent smaller posters and notices, aimed at young children, into the classrooms and corridors of schools.

At the same time, safety issues concerning elderly pedestrians became the focus of a specific campaign targeted at impatient drivers and road users.

Left, above and opposite: Safety posters targeted at pedestrians and drivers.

Polio Awareness

Progress and prosperity after World War II also combined to create new types of risk. The advent of polio vaccination, for example, and its widespread use across juveniles, from the late 1950s onwards, transformed the usual risks attached to youthful adventure.

The dangers of polio were well known. Epidemics associated with the waterborne virus were a recurring feature of most communities in America and Europe from the 1880s onwards. Young children were especially susceptible to the disease, which often resulted in paralysis. Hospital treatment was long, drawn out and involved incarceration within a tank respirator, or iron lung.

These dangers were usually enough to dissuade the young from any contact with standing water. The advent of polio vaccination suddenly made rivers, canals, ponds and lakes fatally attractive. In consequence, there was a spike in the number of water-related accidents and drowning. In the context of the RoSPA archive, from the late 1960s onwards, there are suddenly posters about water safety to address these risks. The risks associated with aquatic adventure were an unintended consequence of medical progress.

Leisure Safety

The society's role in addressing issues of water-based safety increased in proportion to the developing leisure economy in Britain.

Paradoxically, as society was becoming safer, the taste for adventure and extreme sport – boating, surfing, etc – grew more widespread. This resulted in a steady stream of injury and accident, often exacerbated by the fact that incidents were likely to occur in relatively isolated places: out at sea, in reservoirs and so forth.

Also, it does seem as though the 'holiday spirit' makes many of us a little less cautious than when we are at home.

Opposite and below: Water safety posters became increasingly important as more and more people wanted to learn to swim and to enjoy watersports. Overleaf: Safety is just as important on holiday as at home, and the dangers are easily forgotten.

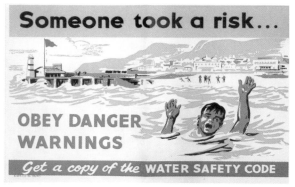

Safety in the Home

Notwithstanding the dangers associated with road use and work, the home has remained a particularly dangerous environment.

Home safety was first addressed by the society during the 1930s. This was a decade when the positive benefits of healthy living conditions began to be expressed through new forms of housing for ordinary people. The post-war template for reconstruction, as evidenced by the new towns, extended the advantages of space, light and air to many more people. At the same time, the home became an increasingly complex and dangerous environment.

The widespread popularity of cigarette smoking contributed to many fire-related accidents in the home. The progressive electrification of the home, and the fact that people began to own a much larger number of electrical machines, also became a source of risk. New standards for electrical wiring and for equipment helped reduce these risks in modern homes, but the danger could not be completely eradicated.

Ironically, the progress toward an increasingly materialistic consumer culture created additional and unforeseen risks. For example, the popularity of venetian and other types of cord-controlled blinds created an additional source of child trauma in the home.

All of these issues have been addressed through various RoSPA campaigns over the past few decades. In general, the society has tackled home safety through the publication of pamphlets and documentation, but the integration of safety advice into the sale and installation of equipment has also helped.

The poster archive contains relatively few posters directed at home safety. In part, this is a reflection of the difficulty of co-ordinating and finding display sites for this kind of material.

Throughout the 1950s and 1960s, industrial safety remained RoSPA's most important area of activity. The framework of safety awareness, which had developed at local level during World War II, remained in place. It was during this period that the poster artist, Leonard Cusden, became the major personality associated with RoSPA's poster material.

During the 1960s and 1970s, British industrial decline and the shift to a post-industrial economy reduced the public perception of the important safety messages. Nevertheless, RoSPA continued to promote safety awareness at work. After the 1980s, the poster format became superseded by a more elaborate variety of training materials that grew to include films, television and video.

By far the most significant factor in the diminished significance of industrial safety

Previous pages and above: Safety in the home.

Right and opposite: Industrial safety begins even before the shift, as the poster opposite shows; and it extends to the smallest instruments and precautions in the workplace itself.

Industrial Safety

The post-war period was an important one for factory and workshop safety in Britain. The role of RoSPA was progressively consolidated by factory safety policy, and the society's agenda was effectively confirmed through legislation.

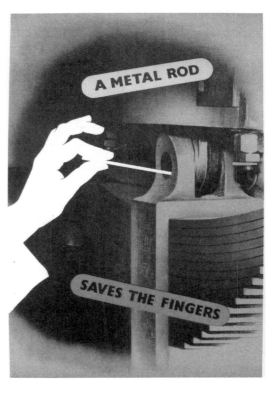

HALT

AT THE
WORKS
GATE

stand from under

Railway Safety

The early history of the railways was a brutal and unforgiving affair. Construction workers died, railway employees died and railway passengers died. The railway also became notorious as the site of unprovoked attack.

The fragmented structure of the early railway industry made it difficult to identify best practice and to enforce a consistent pattern of conduct across the country. The consolidation of the railway industry, in 1923, into four large geographical groups allowed for a more coherent and co-ordinated approach to safety issues on the railway.

was the steady transformation of the working environment from heavy industry to serviced office. By the late 1970s the subscriber base for RoSPA's industrial service had begun to decline, which reflected the steady diminishing of Britain's heavy industrial base and its replacement with, first, a service economy and, secondly, a creative economy. It is fair to say that, within this context, the safety poster became greatly diminished.

These pages and overleaf: A selection of construction and railway safety posters highlighting potentially fatal risks that are easily avoided by taking the most straightforward of precautions.

Previous pages: You're Not Paid to Take Risks; Stand From Under, by Desmond Moore.

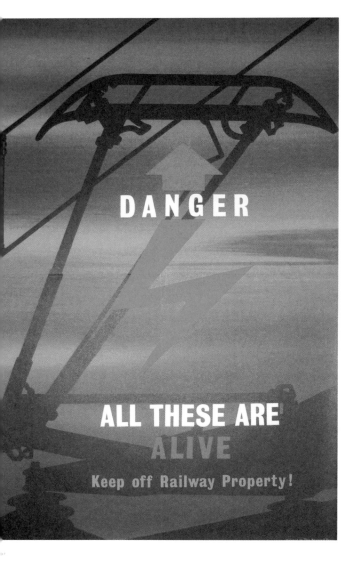

engineering of railway manufacturing also demanded its own specialised posters. Similarly London Transport and the Underground issued their own safety posters.

In these circumstances, it is not surprising that the railways made use of RoSPA's expertise, provided through consultation. A number of RoSPA artists, including Bruce Angrave, Leonard Cusden, Tom Eckersley and HA Rothholz, appeared as part of British Railway's campaign.

Construction Safety

The construction industry faced similar problems to the railways: traditionally, the casual labour employed on site was difficult to engage with consistently, and construction injuries and fatalities tended to be associated with time pressures and the large, heavy machinery used.

The nationalisation of the railway industry after World War II made it simpler still to ensure a consistent expression of safety guidelines. Accordingly, posters addressing various aspects of permanent-way safety were produced. These included posters for passengers and for the public using the railway. Also, there were poster campaigns aimed at railway employees and for the track maintenance teams. The specialised

Like industrial and workshop safety, the society promoted safety through the expression of simple advice and continuous repetition. Within the context of construction site safety there were reminders about the dangers of falling from a height, of carrying too much weight, of not loading properly and of not using machinery as intended.

As the industry consolidated over the years and as projects became bigger in scale, so it became easier to communicate safety messages to workers.

In the special case of recent large civil engineering projects, the combination of scale and public finance have more or less obliged safety routines to be designed into the delivery of projects. The addition of safety protocols into project management has greatly reduced the number of site accidents. So much so, that we are now shocked and horrified when we hear of construction fatalities in the developing world.

These pages: Further examples of railway and construction posters with simple safety messages.

Overleaf: A series of construction safety posters illustrating simple precautions, by Tom Eckersley.

TAKE THE RIGHT STEPS

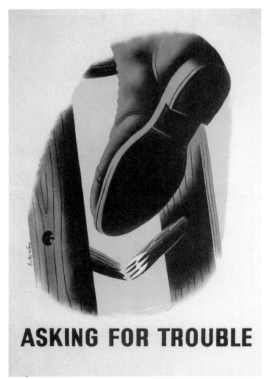

ASKING FOR TROUBLE

STOW TOOLS SAFELY

THINK OF THE MAN BELOW

PREVENT LOOSE HEADS

INSPECT DAILY

STOP !
Look out before crossing

Published by RoSPA (The Royal Society for the Prevention of Accidents), Terminal House, 52 Grosvenor Gardens, London, S.W.1

Printed by Loxley Brothers Limited, London and Sheffield

STJ/144-2

CHAPTER 3

THE CHANGING FACE OF RoSPA

By the late 1960s, RoSPA's poster campaigns had come under threat from a number of practical developments. The advent and success of commercial television provided a hugely efficient means of communication with a mass audience. Simple safety awareness could be integrated, for example, into the everyday narratives of television soaps.

Also, the public spaces in which the posters could be displayed were being tidied up. Typically, RoSPA's road safety campaign posters had been displayed externally on police station sites. The street furniture associated with these displays was tidied away as security issues, especially significant around police stations, became a concern in the late 1970s and 1980s, and to the present.

Migrating the campaigns on to commercial advertising sites was never really an option.

The costs of commercial display were beyond the scope of the organisation, particularly in relation to the kinds of open-ended campaigning associated with road safety.

By the 1980s, RoSPA's poster campaigns had mainly disappeared from public view, except for the annual reminders about the dangers of drinking and driving.

At the same time, RoSPA's industrial safety programme re-focused itself in relation to a wider range of occupational dangers. These tended, as a reflection of the modern post-industrial society, to address issues of emotional stress and tiredness as much as physical safety.

Notwithstanding these changes in background, the simple messages of the society remain as relevant today as ever. Indeed, RoSPA's history shows an organisation

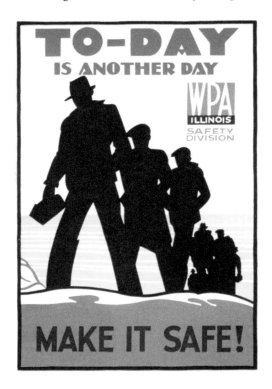

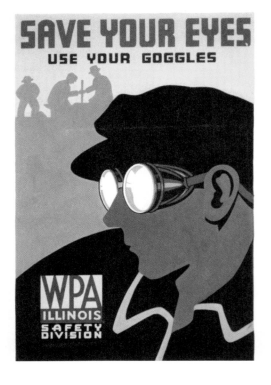

developing from a core activity of industrial, road and home safety into one directing communications across an ever-increasing range of activities.

The success of RoSPA's efforts have also been recognised internationally. The society now acts, in an advisory capacity, with a number of international colleagues.

The World Health Organization (WHO) has identified safety concerns, especially in relation to the rising number of cars in the developing world, as the major challenge of the twenty-first century. Accordingly, the significance of RoSPA's success should be more widely acknowledged.

Safety Campaigns Around the World

The claims I have attached to the historical value of RoSPA's posters, as a consistent and coherent expression of progressive modernism in Britain, can only really be judged in relation to the equivalents from elsewhere.

In itself, this is quite difficult because, for most of the world, there was no platform for the consistent expression of safety messages. Where safety posters did exist, they were often the product of a very particular set of circumstances in that country.

The political situation in Europe between the wars was chaotic and not especially conducive to considerations of worker welfare. In the USSR, for example, worker performance was described entirely in terms of Stakhanovite production targets (the Soviet Stakhanovite movement was a push for workers to over-achieve). In this context, accident prevention was associated with trying to manage the scourge of alcohol abuse within the factory workforce.

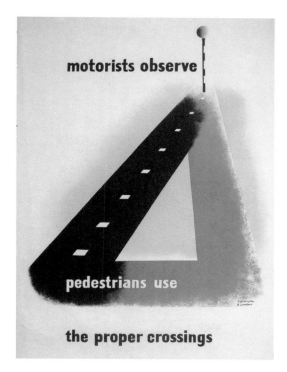

Above: RoSPA encouraged artists to make use of symbols and shapes like the warning triangle within its coordinated poster campaign. Opposite and overleaf: American safety posters tended to stress that safety is the responsibility of the individual.

The concept of worker welfare, as expressed through RoSPA's posters, didn't really exist within the organisation of totalitarian politics. Accordingly, there were few posters concerning worker welfare in Germany during the 1930s, and throughout Europe during World War II. Even after the war, the hierarchical social structures of military dictatorship held back considerations of public safety across southern Europe.

In the USA, safety messages were aligned into a post-crash rhetoric of productive competition. For the US worker, keeping safe was part of an individual responsibility for economic emancipation through productive labour.

Cellar Ceilings must be
FIRE - RETARDED
KEEP CELLARS CLEAN

F. H. LA GUARDIA ··· Mayor   LANGDON W. POST ··· Comm·

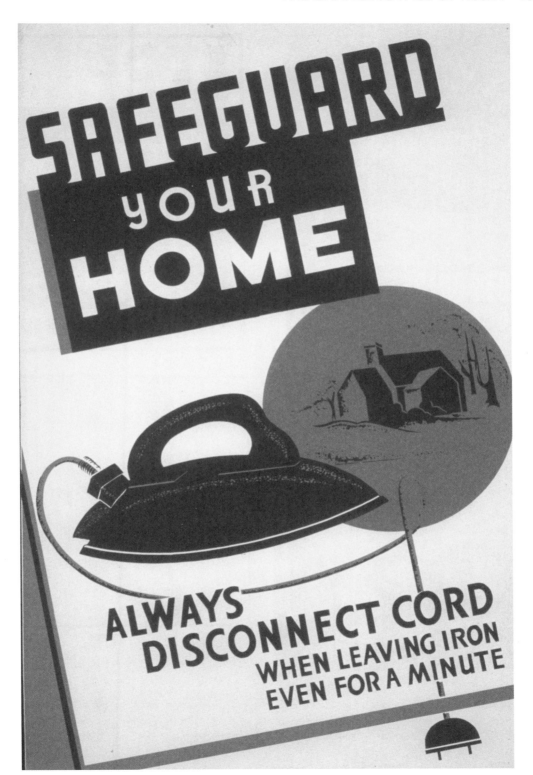

Above: A selection of posters created for the Works Progress Administration, a New Deal employment scheme.
Top left: 'Avoid accidents: Don't stay on the street during an alarm' (1942); Top right: A poster urging caution
against starting forest fires; Bottom left: Against drink-driving ; Bottom right: Construction safety (1937).

In the 1920s, the Chicago printer W Mather began to produce coloured 'Work Incentive' posters. These were distributed on the basis of commercial subscription. The Mather posters espoused good sense and individual responsibility within the American workplace. There was a thinly veiled hostility within the campaign to the idea of organised labour.

Even in France, where visual communication was at its most sophisticated, the consistent promotion of safety only really occurred after World War II: there were construction site and railway safety posters associated with post-war reconstruction. And in the 1970s, France began to address the problem of drinking and driving in rural areas.

In Poland, poster designers embraced the themes of accident prevention, along with making iconoclastic film posters, as a means of expressing a distinct Polish identity through poster design. Furthermore, these images provided an outlet for the expression of a form of resistance to the overbearing imposition of Soviet hegemony.

In Switzerland from the 1950s onwards, the expression of ideas through graphic design was systematised into a coherent and consistent engagement with the world. The expression of institutional organisation was quickly extended to provide for safety within town, commune and workplace.

Against this patchy and inconsistent background, the RoSPA posters look especially interesting: they were the first of their kind and they embraced modern techniques of graphic communication.

In the context of promoting safety awareness, it seems that continuous repetition provides for the most likely success.

Below: A promotional catalogue of safety posters available from the NSFA during the 1930s and a RoSPA safe driving badge.

A Century of Safety Poster Success

The safety posters presented in this book provide graphic and visual testimony to RoSPA's posters over the last one hundred years. The posters are remarkably consistent and coherent in their expression of simple messages. The more or less continuous repetition of these messages has had a profound impact on the working lives of millions of Britons. This is worth celebrating.

But the posters also offer an alternative perspective upon RoSPA. Its founding principles, along with the backgrounds and personalities of the major protagonists, suggest an organisation aligned with the most progressive elements in British design politics.

The association of graphic design and progressive ideas evidenced by these posters provide substantive proof of a wide-ranging acceptance of modernist ideas in twentieth-century Britain.

Over the years, the consistently repeated safety messages have provided a verifiable pattern of safety against which our individual engagement with the mechanised world can be judged. The posters literally translate into a routine pattern of behaviour that keeps individuals and families safe.

The economic, social and political benefits of this branch of poster design have been enormous. In the twenty-first century, we have the opportunity to be grateful for this work and to celebrate the very substantial achievement

Opposite and below: The changing face of RoSPA in the 1960s and '70s, with posters addressing driver and pedestrian awareness. Overleaf: Children and road safety – a perennial RoSPA topic.

of RoSPA. We can only hope that these efforts may continue and this example is followed throughout the developing world.

RoSPA Today

RoSPA in the twenty-first century remains at the heart of accident prevention in the UK – though this does not mean that the organisation campaigns for 'absolute safety'. Instead, it takes the thoroughly practical and realistic view that our lives should be as safe as necessary, not as safe as possible; that good accident prevention is about managing risk safely, rather than banning potentially hazardous activities altogether.

The organisation still runs campaigns on the key issues that it has been involved with over the last century, namely workplace, road, home, leisure and education safety. However, RoSPA continually adapts to our changing world. The most recent campaigns have focused on areas such as window-blind cords, driveway safety, young drivers and safer electric gates. RoSPA's Lighter Evenings campaign has also proposed the amendment of Britain's system of changing the clocks in winter and summer, arguing that such a change would not only improve road safety, but would also bring a host of other benefits, including increases in tourism, leisure time and wellbeing.

RoSPA's methods of raising awareness are now wide-ranging and embrace modern technology channels. The organisation runs a vast array of training courses, utilising both traditional classroom teaching and e-learning. It also produces extensive resources for parents, teachers and employers; provides health and safety consultancy and audit services; and collaborates with partners across Europe and around the world.

In short, the modern-day RoSPA is engaged in a huge range of activities and its remit now stretches far beyond what would have been envisaged a century ago. But ultimately, its mission remains the same: to save lives and reduce injuries.

Opposite and below: Our changing society – including roles of women at home and in the workplace – have been reflected in RoSPA's poster output through the decades. Overleaf: Messages about home safety and first aid are as relevant today as at any time through RoSPA's history.

Jenny says **BE SMART DRESS SAFELY FOR WORK**

we all shoulder a responsibility for safety

CHAPTER 4

THE DESIGN
& PRINTING
OF THE POSTERS

The overarching history of RoSPA and the safety messages it disseminated are but one part of the story of the poster archive. This chapter celebrates some of the brilliant designers and the printing firm behind the posters, before exploring the technical side of the posters' production.

The Designers

The contemporary practice of graphic design hardly existed in Britain before World War II. Indeed, the term was only coined, in Britain at least, after the war. Before then, there were commercial artists, illustrators and a few specialist poster designers working for the larger printing houses. In consequence, their work tended towards a generic form of commercial image-making derived from what was already around. In any event, their work was entirely embedded within the world of printing and design.

During the 1930s a small number of artist-designers began to work independently and to think beyond the appearance of their work, and to consider the possible meanings attached to images. This conceptual thinking was extremely useful to the nascent advertising industry and, later, to the Ministry of Information during World War II.

Thus, the graphic designer emerged: a professional communications expert adept at combining image and text.

Some of these new graphic designers worked on the RoSPA posters. Therefore, the discovery of the archive fills a gap in our knowledge of design history in Britain. In the first place, the institutional framework behind the posters' origins adds substantially to our understanding of British modernism before World War II.

Secondly, the roll call of designers used in the campaigns includes some well-known names and increases our knowledge of independent practitioners during the 1940s and 1950s. A number of these personalities were émigré designers from Europe. In addition, a shared background in non-conformism distinguishes many of the British artist-designers.

Bruce Angrave

Born in Leicester, Bruce Angrave studied at Chiswick Art School, Ealing School of Art and the Central School of Art, London. He worked as a freelance book illustrator and periodical

that the appropriate consignment notes are correctly completed and agree with goods in number and condition

Left and opposite: Bruce Angrave often used words as integral and effective elements of his poster design.

illustrator, designer and paper-sculptor (including paper works for the Festival of Britain in 1951 and Expo '70 in Japan). Angrave was a member of the Society of Industrial Artists (SIA) and his poster designs were influenced by Tom Eckersley, 'Lewitt-Him' and Abram Games.

Cyril Kenneth Bird, aka 'Fougasse'

During the 1930s, the society's road safety message was communicated through a series of drawings and pamphlets designed by Cyril Kenneth Bird.

His posters exemplify the popular and widespread use of humour in visual propaganda.

Opposite and below: Posters by Fougasse promoting vehicle maintenance and awareness of pedestrians.

Bird's famous *Careless Talk Costs Lives* anti-rumour posters, designed in 1939, showed Hitler and Goering materialising from man-hole openings and telephone boxes, in clubs, pubs and teashops. Hitler was drawn, in comic style, as a pipsqueak in Ruritanian uniform with medals, whilst Goering was portrayed as his overweight sidekick. Together, they were a 'little-and-large' comic double-act, recognisable to everyone as a staple of British music hall and comic theatre. In fact, Fougasse had already perfected this double-act in the context of his road safety commentary.

Fougasse's approach to design and communication was informed by his own observation that the conditions for successful propaganda are not auspicious: people are disinclined to read any notice and are further disinclined to believe that anything they read applies to them. Lastly, they are unwilling to recall any message long enough to act upon it.

Fougasse identified that the strategy most likely to succeed, therefore, was one of attraction, persuasion and action. Communication success required each of these elements to be addressed in a coherent and functional manner and, crucially, joined together into a single, coherent, design.

The appeal, through wit, of the *Careless Talk* message, was crucial. In the first instance, the posters appealed to those places expected to display them. As Fougasse rightly understood, it was unreasonable to expect 'the owners of teashops, restaurants or public houses to put up horror propaganda for their clients' comfort'. Given the choice between gruesome pictorial warnings and the opportunity to entertain their clients, most would usually choose the latter.

"But I keep on telling you the brakes used to hold all right"

HOW ARE YOUR BRAKES —— & TYRES?

Issued by the National Safety First Association
Terminal House, 52 Grosvenor Gardens, London. S.W.1

The appeal to humour also allowed a space for the viewer. Usually, this involved recognising a connection, or humorous disconnect, between what was being shown and what was being suggested. The development of graphic wit was crucial in sustaining the longevity of these messages.

After World War I, Bird became a jobbing artist specialising in humour, which led to a series of illustrations on the emerging protocols of safe, courteous driving. They reveal an appreciation of the slightly ridiculous nature of the many rules and regulations that govern British life and, especially, middle-class society. The Fougasse treatment of these social protocols was, though, more benign than that favoured by HM Bateman or David Low, for example.

Fougasse extended his system of presentation, pioneered in relation to the emerging rules of the road, to apply variously to the protocols of bridge parties and of behaviour in London's Underground.

Frederick Donald Blake

Scotsman Frederick Donald Blake lived in the south of England for most of his life. He trained at Camberwell School of Art and at fifteen years of age started work as an architectural draughtsman in the interior design business.

Early in 1940, he was drafted into a small group of war artists producing propaganda work for the Ministry of Information. On the other nights he worked long hours as an Air Raid Fire Officer. During this period he began to exhibit his paintings. He had work shown at the Royal Academy together with other open exhibitions in London.

As a freelance designer after the war, he worked for the aircraft industry, the railways and on RoSPA's campaigns.

Above: A poster by the prolific and highly influential Leonard Cusden.

Opposite: 'Don't Lose Sight of Them': an eye safety poster by Frederick Blake.

Leonard Cusden

Leonard Cusden enjoyed a long and distinguished association with RoSPA. He eventually became creative director and adviser for the organisation.

GOOD STACKS

don't fall

Above: A simple but extremely effective design by Leonard Cusden.
Opposite: 'Wait Till it Stops' by Robin Day.

Cusden was born in Ireland and began to design posters during the 1930s. His commercial designs were in the flat-colour style of golden-age railway posters. The economic constraints associated with RoSPA's campaigns suggested further simplification would be an advantage and Cusden became a master of working within these financial constraints.

Roland Davies

In the 1950s, Roland Davies produced many dramatic posters for RoSPA's road safety campaigns. He first studied to be a lithographer, but became an illustrator instead, starting with cinema posters and illustrations for magazines. He worked in a dramatic and naturalistic style.

Robin Day

Best known as a pioneer furniture designer of the post-war period in Britain, Robin Day began his professional career in exhibition design and poster design. Between 1948 and 1949 he designed posters for RAF recruitment and for exhibitions. His work was included in the Low Cost Furniture exhibition, held at the Museum of Modern Art, New York, in 1948.

Day's RoSPA posters date from a short period at the beginning of his career.

Tom Eckersley

Tom Eckersley designed a number of posters for RoSPA during World War II and he was also a member of its post-war poster committee.

Eckersley was able, through the various opportunities of his long career, to make several distinct contributions to the development of graphic design in Britain.

He was born into a nonconformist family in Manchester and was repeatedly poorly as a young child. His interest in drawing came, in part at least, as a benefit of the subsequent occupational therapy and rehabilitation. From 1930 to 1934, he attended Salford School of Art, where he met Eric Lombers and the two began to design posters together. They were awarded the Heywood Medal at the school and the pair quickly established themselves as poster designers in London. From 1935 onwards, they received a steady flow of commissions from the major patrons of poster art.

The advent of World War II caused the design partnership to break up. Eckersley joined the RAF, where his drawing skills were used in cartography. He also found that he could visualise a poster design whilst drawing for the RAF and produce it whilst on leave. By this means he was able to fulfil various commissions, including those for RoSPA.

After the war, Eckersley joined the London College of Printing, where he was instrumental in establishing the first courses in graphic design.

Eckersley's remarkable sixty-year career also included a long-lasting creative relationship with London Transport.

Abram Games

Abram Games is widely regarded as Britain's most significant poster designer during World War II. He began his career in the 1930s and was quickly recognised as a poster artist with strong visual ideas and as a master of the airbrush.

The desperate circumstances of war convinced Games that the military authorities required new forms of visual communication as a matter of urgency. He was appointed Official War Office Poster Designer in 1941. The eventual promotion to the commissioned rank of Captain was an acknowledgement, by the military, of his amazing contribution.

Throughout the war, Games produced a prodigious number of poster designs aimed at helping his fellow soldiers. Some of the messages were simple attempts to deal with the practicalities of military life. Others were more idealistic and pointed to the political and democratic consequences of the war. Games always tried to use minimum means to maximum effect. He developed a unique way of combining two visual ideas, so as to make the connection explicit.

The procedure was an evolution of the surrealist techniques of transformation that had been introduced to the visual language of poster design by Paul Nash. Generally though, surrealist transformations were too subtle for military communications.

Above: Abram Games's work was a major influence on Bruce Angrave.

Opposite: A cycle safety poster by Tom Eckersley, dating from 1947, when the artist was also undertaking book illustration commissions.

Accordingly, Games combined transformation with visual simplification, based on the example of Edward McKnight Kauffer. Games understood the visual impact of scaling, colour and simplification that Kauffer had introduced in the 1930s. The result was a new and powerful extension to the visual language and intellectual range of poster communication.

F Kenwood Giles

Kenwood Giles was an illustrator and designer who contributed humorous designs for RoSPA.

Edward McKnight Kauffer

Edward McKnight Kauffer, an American artist and poster designer, made a crucial contribution to design in Britain during the period before World War II with his Safety Week posters.

Kauffer was born into the relative isolation of the American mid-west. His precocious artistic talent first expressed itself through sketching and painting. In 1913 Kauffer travelled to Europe and found himself in London at the outbreak of war. The city proved attractive to Kauffer: the general cultural atmosphere was more advanced and adventurous than in Chicago whilst, at the same time, appearing less obviously intimidating than that which he had encountered in Munich and Paris.

In an effort to support himself he began to search out poster commissions and other design work. A meeting with the illustrator John Hassall, in 1915, provided him with an introduction to Frank Pick, a founder member of the Design and Industries Association.

The circuitous route by which Kauffer and Pick came to meet is important because it describes the combination of influences that Kauffer brought to poster design after 1915. His beginnings as a theatrical scenery painter in America provided him with a clear sense of how scale, colour and simplification could be combined effectively. In Europe, Kauffer immediately responded to the visual simplifications of Ludwig Hohlwein's poster designs in Munich. By the time Kauffer reached Britain, he was familiar with a wide range of artistic ideas from across Europe.

Kauffer's instinctive disposition towards the scale and drama of the poster, along with his conceptual and artistic sophistication, was unusual in Britain. The combination was attractive to Pick, who was committed to improving general standards of design. Pick immediately began to commission poster designs from the young American. In the end, Kauffer and Pick worked together until 1939.

Kauffer provided a new kind of bridge between the separate worlds of fine art and poster design. The first artists to attempt poster design had, typically, simply produced their usual work in poster form. Kauffer was able, by temperament and opportunity, to develop a visual language that synthesised

Left: Pat Keely's simple two-colour factory-safety poster. Opposite: Stan Krol's 'Falls are not Funny'.

a number of different visual elements from modern art into poster design. By producing, over time, a coherent visual language that combined colour, scale, abstraction, simplification and integration, Kauffer was able to advance the scope of poster communication beyond the prosaic demands of the advertising industry.

Suddenly, posters appeared bigger and brighter and more audacious.

Posters by 'Lewitt-Him' (below), Philip Mendoza (opposite) and Desmond Moore (overleaf).

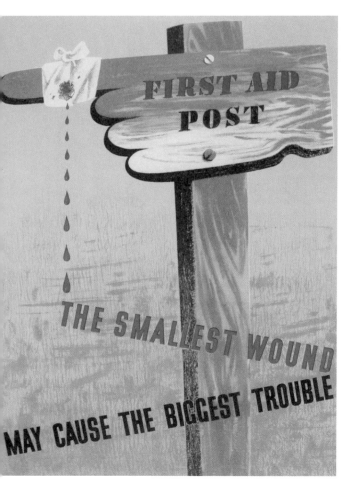

Pat Keely

Patrick Keely established himself as a successful poster designer during the 1920s. His first designs were for the Southern Railway in 1928. Thereafter he also produced designs for the GPO and for London Underground. During World War II he worked for both the Ministry of Information and for RoSPA.

His propaganda designs were distinguished by a group of posters that he designed for display in Holland. Keely seems to have withdrawn from design after about 1950.

Stan Krol

A poster designer for both London Transport and RoSPA, Stan Krol appears to have been active from the mid-1950s until the 1970s.

Theyre Lee-Elliott

During the 1930s and 1940s, Theyre Lee-Elliott pioneered a form of modernist information design, which proved an especially valuable support to the advocates of scientific management and operational research within large organisations.

Jan Lewitt and George Him, aka 'Lewitt-Him'

Jan Lewitt and George Him were Polish émigré designers who arrived in Britain at the end of the 1930s. They are probably best known for their work as book illustrators during the 1940s.

Their poster work during World War II was distinguished by a highly developed sense of visual wit. They produced many poster designs for the GPO during the 1950s. George Him became a senior figure in Britain's design establishment during the later 1950s.

Philip Mendoza

A stalwart of various RoSPA campaigns during World War II, Philip Mendoza's dramatic cartoon drawing style combined humour with simplicity and legibility. It was ideal for RoSPA's illustrated books featuring Percy Vere, the hapless worker.

Arthur Mills

Arthur Mills designed a small number of posters for RoSPA during World War II.

Desmond Moore

Desmond Moore was a member of the technical staff at the London College of Printing and was a close friend of Tom Eckersley. He produced a small number of poster designs for RoSPA during World War II.

GR Morris

The American designer GR Morris is first recorded as a contributor to the advertising campaign of Shell-Mex and BP during 1938. His work for RoSPA during World War II was remarkable for its sophisticated use of photographic elements in poster design. Tom Eckersley included several designs by Morris as illustrations for his book *Poster Design*, from 1954. This is evidence of the esteem in which these designs were held.

No record exists of Morris designs after the end of the war. His career seems to have foundered as a consequence of an addictive personality disorder.

Peter Ray

Peter Ray designed the typographic slogan posters for RoSPA. In the early twentieth century, typography remained an obscure and specialised area of printing and design. By the 1940s, typographic convention had developed through the arts-and-crafts stage, machine setting, asymmetric setting and the return to classicism.

Ray counts as one of a relatively small group of named typographers working at that time.

Ray's professional activities extended to the senior position of Honorary Secretary within the Society of Industrial Artists. Ray was instrumental, as editor, in the publication of *Designers in Britain* (1947). The society published surveys of British design by its members at two-yearly intervals.

DESMOND MOORE, 45

MADE TO MEASURE

RIGHT SPANNER-RIGHT NUT

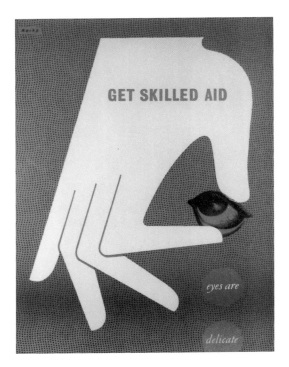

GET SKILLED AID

eyes are

delicate

Manfred Reiss

Born in Leipzig, Germany, Manfred Reiss moved to London in 1937, along with his family and forty Jewish children from the local community.

In London, Reiss pursued a successful career in graphic design. In the late 1940s and early 1950s he was one of the most prolific British poster designers and many of his creations were reproduced in the *International Poster Annuals*, a selection of the best poster designs from around the world at the time. Reiss' posters were always cleanly designed and easy to understand, often composed of simple drawings with a photo-montage or simple photographed elements.

HA Rothholz

Hans Arnold Rothholz came to Britain from Germany in 1933 and soon adopted the name 'Arnold' in everyday use (he usually signed his posters 'HA Rothholz', although he also sometimes used the initials 'AR', or the abbreviation 'Roth'). As a teenager, he attended Willesden School of Art and his career was interrupted by the outbreak of World War II, when he was interned and subsequently deported to Canada by the British authorities. His designs for RoSPA therefore come from the very beginning of the war or from its end.

He worked as a poster designer, graphic designer and advertising art director. Later, he produced a set of accident prevention posters for British Rail.

Harry Rowntree

New Zealander Harry Rowntree was a distinguished and successful children's book illustrator. He contributed to RoSPA's illustrational campaigns.

Hans Schleger, aka 'Zero'

A German graphic designer who came to Britain in 1932, Hans Schleger worked for London Transport and for the NSFA Safety Week campaigns during the 1930s. He is credited with helping to introduce sophisticated continental ideas – surrealism and modernism in design, especially – to Britain. He also designed road safety posters for RoSPA after World War II.

Schleger was an important pioneer of design integration and corporate identity. He remains a very important figure in the development of modernist graphic communication in Britain.

George Smith, aka 'Gus'

A regular designer for RoSPA from the 1950s onwards, George Smith was also a newspaper cartoonist.

Posters by Manfred Reiss (opposite), HA Rothholz (above), and 'Gus' (overleaf).

LO K THROUGH
FIRST

RoSPA's Printers

The firm of Loxley Brothers in Sheffield had a close and important relationship with RoSPA as it printed all of the society's posters over a number of decades.

The history of Loxley Brothers is closely associated with the Quaker and Yorkshire non-conformist traditions of enterprise and welfare.

According to the authorised history of the firm (written by Mary Walton in 1954 and held in Sheffield City Library), Loxley Brothers was founded by Edward and William Loxley in 1854. From the first, the printing firm was closely associated with employee welfare. In the 1860s, this took the form of cricket matches between the works team and local opponents. The Atlas Works team was based at Bramhall Lane, Sheffield, now home of Sheffield United Football Club. The firm's sporting efforts were part of a wider movement that established football and cricket as national games.

By the end of the nineteenth century, Loxley Brothers was successfully established and the company resolved to expand to a regional or even national scale. This process began with the acquisition of Sheffield Independent Printers – a large general printing firm – and the appointment of JB Morrell, of York, as chairman of the new firm.

Morrell was well known in Yorkshire as a director of Rowntree, the York-based confectionery firm of Quaker origins. He was also an alderman of the city and Lord Mayor. Morrell is credited with having turned Loxley Brothers into a printing firm of national scale and reach.

SAFETY WEEK REMINDERS
FOR MASS ADVERTISING

The design shown here in full colour is now available in two special sizes as useful adjuncts to the Safety Week posters recently produced by RoSPA for the Ministry of Labour and National Service. Both sizes have a space in the bottom right-hand corner so that the date of the Safety Week may be inserted.

MINIPOSTERS—size 11½" × 7½" are for general use about the works in situations which cannot carry a full-sized 20" × 30" bill, e.g., on stanchions, plants, waste-bins, etc., and also on or near danger points.

STICKIBACKS—size approximately 1¾" × 1½", are printed in sheets of 40 on perforated and gummed paper. They are for use not only on correspondence and other stationery but also during inspections, when they may be stuck on parts of the plant to draw attention to points needing correction.

PRICES
(including postage)

Miniposters		Stickibacks	
One dozen	3s. 6d.	Sheet of 40 stamps	2s. 0d.
Fifty	12s. 6d.	Six sheets (240 stamps)	10s. 6d.
Hundred	22s. 6d.	Twelve sheets (480 stamps)	20s.

The above prices may be subject to a slight alteration after April 1st 1946

ORDER FORM OVERLEAF

It was Morrell who saw the possibilities of growing the Loxley business through expansion, acquisition and consolidation. He was also able, through his business connections, to raise the necessary capital for this plan. So successful was he that he was still in the chair for the centenary celebrations of 1954.

The years 1920 and 1921 were very active for Loxley Brothers. The firm purchased the printing firms of British Periodicals Ltd, St Dunstan's Press, Cornish Press and Garden City Press, based in Letchworth Garden City, Hertfordshire.

The association with Garden City Press was both practical and symbolic. The business was primarily a book printer and binding works, which was obviously of great use. But given Loxley's pioneering role in worker welfare,

it was also entirely appropriate that the firm should be represented within the model and garden city environment, as conceptualised by Ebenezer Howard and Henrietta Barnett. The firm's location in Letchworth aligned it with the pioneering, Quaker, efforts at business reform. New employees were given a six-month training period and then, if successful, were taken on, and given the status of owner-workers within the firm.

The Loxley enterprise remained busy with a steady flow of flat printing, in colour, for Rowntree's point-of-sale advertising and packaging. This work was the platform from which the growth of the business could be projected. In 1921, all the printing operations were consolidated into the New Atlas Works at Aizelwood Road.

In December 1923, a fire destroyed the new works, but by August 1925, the Aizelwood Road works were open for business again,

These pages: RoSPA's posters, leaflets and wage-packet 'slogan slips' added up to a lot of printing.

WALKERS RIDERS DRIVERS

CONCENTRATE

WHEN USING THE ROADS

equipped with Crabtree offset-lithographic machines (see 'Printing the Posters' on page 130). It was these machines, and their potential for the quick, high-volume colour work, that recommended Loxley Brothers to RoSPA.

By the end of the 1920s, Loxley Brothers' own publicity described their activities as specialising in catalogues, brochures, house magazines and general high-class letterpress work, lithographic printing in colour and labels, posters, show cards and general advertising.

The relationship between RoSPA and Loxley began during the 1930s. The exact circumstances behind the relationship remain slightly obscure although the firm was, by that time, equipped with high-speed two-colour lithographic presses. Accordingly, they could complete the work quickly and economically. The central location of the firm, in Sheffield, was also convenient as a base for the distribution of RoSPA material to subscribers, many of which were based in the industrial heartlands of northern England and the Midlands.

Loxley Brothers printed all of RoSPA's posters during World War II and against a background of paper shortages and austerity. During the war, RoSPA posters were printed double-sided and in a narrow-portrait format for economy. The industrial safety campaigns, which were underwritten by the Ministry of Labour, grew rapidly in size and became the largest of RoSPA's activities.

After the war, RoSPA's poster requirements again grew substantially and Loxley with them. Throughout the 1950s and 1960s, the industrial safety campaigns remained the most significant of RoSPA's, and Loxley's, activities. By the 1970s, the road safety campaigns had become substantially more important and rivalled the scale of the industrial service. In addition, RoSPA's activities were now extended to cover a raft of new campaigns.

The RoSPA account and its poster subscriptions remained the most substantial part of Loxley's activities until the 1990s.

Above and below: two colours; opposite: three.

Printing the Posters

RoSPA's posters were printed using 'two-colour photo-mechanical offset-litho'. But what does this mean? This tongue-twisting description is probably incomprehensible to anyone not already involved in printing and design. Furthermore, since the advent of digital technology, the phrase describes an historic form of technology and organisation specific to the middle of the twentieth century. So, even if you know about present-day printing and communication, this phrase may be a little unclear. Accordingly, this section describes the terms, techniques and process behind the printing of RoSPA's posters.

These pages: two-colour posters printed in black and red inks by offset litho.

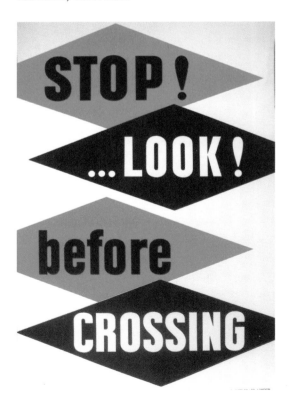

The phrase 'two-colour photo-mechanical offset-litho' actually comprises three separate and distinct terms that describe the technology, process and specification of what is being done.

'Offset-litho' refers to a development of lithography whereby the addition of an offset roller into the print machinery allowed for a simplification and acceleration of the printing process. The term 'offset' may be understood as distinguishing an up-to-date and efficient form of high-volume printing.

Lithography was a unique form of printing, developed by Aloys Senefelder at the very end of the eighteenth century. The process devolved from the antipathy of oil and water and allowed for a print to be taken from a flat surface.

GUARD
OPEN
FIRES

Issued by the Royal Society for the Prevention of Accidents, Terminal House, 52, Grosvenor Gardens, London, S.W.1.

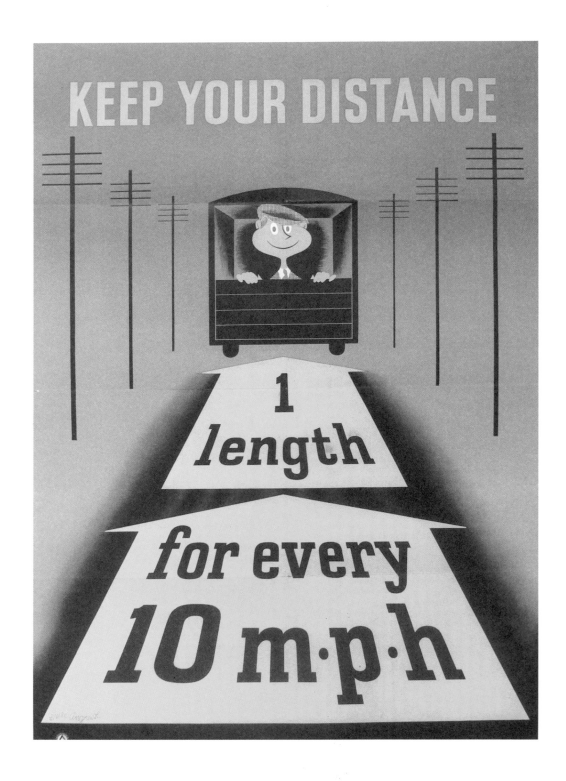

Before lithography, printing always involved variations on the 'intaglio' or 'relief' processes. Intaglio printing involved filling an engraved mark with ink and pressing paper into an engraved plate. Relief printing will be more familiar to most people; it is the basic method of letterpress printing and potato-prints. The plate is cut away to leave high points that may be inked so as to produce an image from this high relief.

In contrast, lithography simply involved drawing on the flat surface of stone or metal. The use of a special greasy crayon allowed for ink to attach to the drawn areas of the plate and to be washed away from the remaining area. Subsequently, a print may be taken by contact with a flat surface.

These pages: The use of bold, flat colours in poster design made for a more manageable production process than photographic plates in pre-digital days.

The development of lithography transformed the mechanics of printing. The flat surface of the plate allowed for a print to be made from just a contact, rather than from contact and pressure. The reduction in mechanical forces associated with the traditional printing press allowed for much larger surface areas to be printed.

The scaling effects made possible by lithography led to the elaboration of new kinds of print display. Lithographic drawing also allowed for a more complete integration of word and image. The modern poster, for example – distinguished by scale, colour and design integration – was made possible by the machinery of lithography.

Printing inks don't dry straight away. Wet inks may easily transfer to other surfaces. All printers know to avoid this when stacking freshly printed work. Offset was developed from this tendency of printing inks to transfer from paper to other surfaces.

The problems of water and offset suggested an improvement to the print mechanism of the litho press. A rubber blanket could be made to pick up and transfer the printed areas of the plate and to offset this onto the paper to produce the print. In the first instance, the offset blanket kept water, plate and paper separate. Later, special rubber compounds were developed to further help keep water and ink separate.

These pages: Areas of solid colour place pressure on the paper surface, making paper quality important.

All printing is a form of magic; but lithography is especially impressive. It seems improbable and incomprehensible until one sees it demonstrated. The process is simple, and works beautifully.

Early lithographers were confronted by a number of problems deriving from the mechanics of the process. For example, the process of washing away surplus ink from the plate or stone produced a volume of water that could quickly compromise the integrity of the paper stock. Indeed, Senefelder identified stone and metal as the best materials from which litho prints could be taken, precisely because they were resistant to water. Nevertheless, the quality of printing required that water, ink and paper be kept apart as much as possible and that their interaction be precisely controlled.

The soft contact between the offset blanket and inked plate helped to ensure the integrity of the print design. This was especially important for those branches of printing concerned with the production of packaging and display items.

The addition of offset also produced several other important changes to the lithographic process. The offset blanket was quickly superseded by a roller mechanism. This had the advantage of speeding up the press mechanism. Indeed, the shift from flatbed to rotary action was a general characteristic of mechanisation and increased efficiency in print machinery. The addition of another surface into the print process also allowed for the original plate drawing to be made as a positive, rather than a negative. By the end of the

nineteenth century, lithographic drawing had developed so as to become a specialised skill of drawing out colour separations, by hand and in reverse, for each part of the print. This was time-consuming and expensive. So, the offset process was both an efficiency gain and a cost saving to lithographic printers.

In its original form, lithography was conceived as a single-colour process. The commercial development of lithography quickly led to the elaboration of colour printing. In simple terms, this involved a separate printing for each colour and for all the make-ready (preparing a press) and studio operations required to support the consecutive printing of all the different elements of a design. So, a four-colour design was actually much more than four times the work of producing a single-colour design.

show you're moving
switch on
HEADLIGHTS
STOP
ACCIDENTS on the road

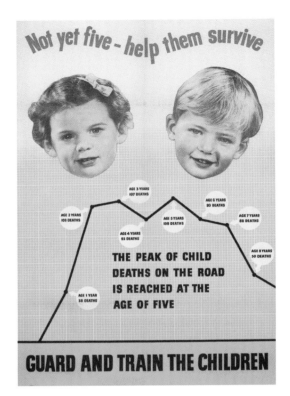

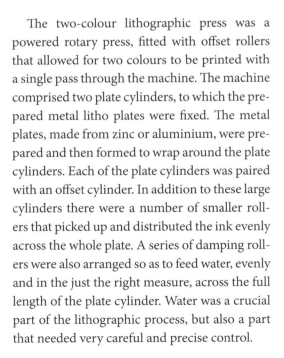

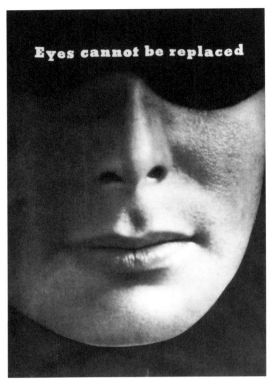

The two-colour lithographic press was a powered rotary press, fitted with offset rollers that allowed for two colours to be printed with a single pass through the machine. The machine comprised two plate cylinders, to which the prepared metal litho plates were fixed. The metal plates, made from zinc or aluminium, were prepared and then formed to wrap around the plate cylinders. Each of the plate cylinders was paired with an offset cylinder. In addition to these large cylinders there were a number of smaller rollers that picked up and distributed the ink evenly across the whole plate. A series of damping rollers were also arranged so as to feed water, evenly and in the just the right measure, across the full length of the plate cylinder. Water was a crucial part of the lithographic process, but also a part that needed very careful and precise control.

The arrangement of cylinders and rollers was generally stacked vertically to produce a machine with a compact footprint within the workshop. In contrast, four-colour, Heidelberg-style presses were usually laid out as a horizontal series of cylinders; one each for cyan, magenta, yellow and key (black) printings. Nowadays, this is known as CMYK.

The term 'photo-mechanical' describes how the make-ready of the press was carried out according to a series of mechanical processes. That doesn't mean that the process was mechanised. It means that the tasks of the process were carried out according to technical norms and specifications. In the first instance, this allowed the work of colour separation (before plates were made) to be done by using coloured filters. The interpretation of design

These pages: Poster designs from different eras showing the evolution of printing from one to two and then four colours, and plate-making from photographic subject matter as well as illustration.

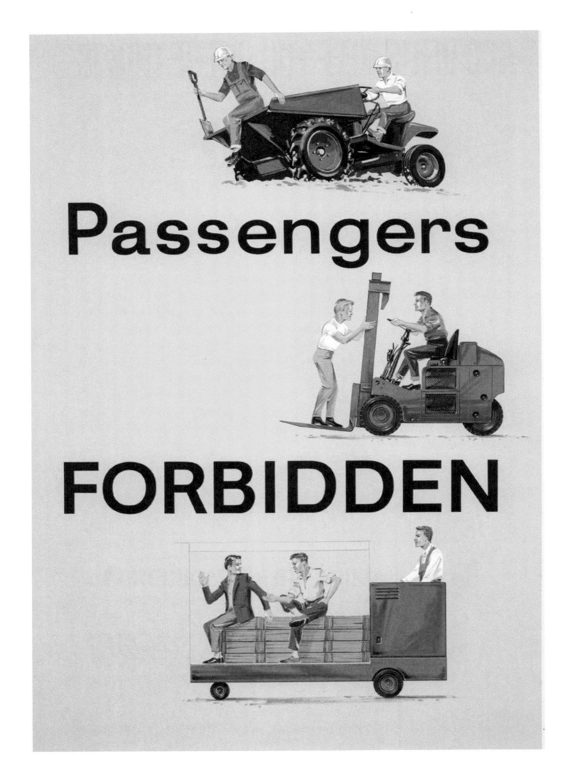

Passengers

FORBIDDEN

according to subjective and craft judgement was replaced by a series of technical steps that could be exactly, and objectively, described by the numeric values of aperture settings and exposure.

Putting all these terms together describes, to print technicians and graphic designers at least, a technical process and a standard of output that was defined by a series of mechanical steps. That doesn't mean that the process was entirely automated. But it does describe a process where each step was defined by numerically defined technical parameters rather than craft-based and subjective judgements.

Notwithstanding the advancing automation of the print industry at the time, there remained several areas of human expertise. In the print shop, the machine minding was instrumental in the efficient running of the whole workshop. The success of any print enterprise required that the machine presses were running at capacity. Any delay or stoppage in printing compromised the economic integrity of the works.

The basic roles of machine minding were to manage paper and ink so that speed and quality were optimised. Lithographic inks were usually supplied in the form of thick paste. This was thinned and introduced into the machine via a trough located along the front of the machine. The inking rollers were arranged in sequence, so that their action spread the ink evenly across the full width of the machine. The ink had to rest on the print so that it dried quickly and minimised the risk of offset, or of prints sticking to each other. Accordingly, machine speed, efficiency and print quality were each linked to this ostensibly simple, but important, action.

Depending on the design of the poster, the ink trough could also provide a means for printing additional colours through the so-called 'split-duct' process. This involved dividing the ink trough through the erection of a partition across the trough. Differently coloured inks could then be placed in the trough and to each side of the partition. Accordingly, and at optimum speed, two colours would be printed, simultaneously, and in one pass through the machine. Thus a two-colour machine could be transformed into a three- or four-colour machine.

Obviously, this mechanical sleight-of-hand required that the inks be kept separate, and this had to be reflected in the design of the poster. A number of RoSPA designers, Tom Eckersley and Leonard Cusden amongst them, became adept at working to specification.

Previous pages and these pages: A selection of posters from different eras that were designed, illustrated, prepared for platemaking and printed with different techniques.

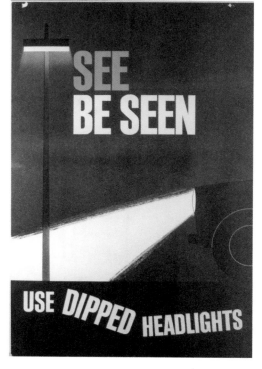

The design of the poster was usually presented as painted artwork. This was prepared in actual size, or in the correct aspect ratio for enlargement to the standard 30" x 20" (double crown) size. Photographic elements were included as collaged elements in the artwork.

The make-ready for printing involved preparing the colour separations and different plates required for printing. Each colour in the design required its own printing plate. The colour separations could be made relatively easily, using the photo studio, coloured filters and the darkroom. The separation could then be transferred to a thick glass plate and the design permanently rendered in liquid opaque. These glass plates, in actual size, could be retained for subsequent printings.

Laying the glass over a zinc printing plate (prepared with a light-sensitive emulsion) and exposing it to light allowed for a precise transfer of the design to be made quickly. This process is familiar to anyone who has worked in a black-and-white darkroom.

The finishing of the posters allowed for any trimming and folding operations. The posters were usually folded, twice, so that they could be easily stored, identified and sent out in standard sized postal envelopes.

These pages: However automated the process, the final adjustments to ensure colour fidelity across the print run and among posters in each series rested with skilled machine minders.

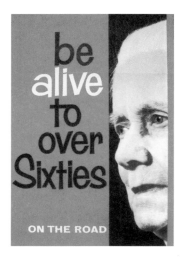

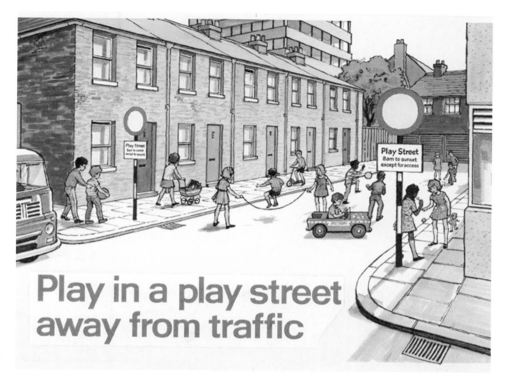

Above: Stan Krol's poster dates from the 1960s, but it reprises one of RoSPA's earliest messages concerning pedestrian safety during the wartime blackouts. Opposite: Another 1960s poster, this time by 'Gus', promotes tidy – and thus, safer – workplace practices. The poster carries a subtext that management should train juniors in safe working routines.

▶ Key Dates in RoSPA's History ————————▶

1916 A public meeting at Caxton Hall in London discusses the 'alarming increase in traffic accidents, and the direct connection therewith of the restricted street lighting which had been necessitated by the War conditions.' The meeting decides to elect a London 'Safety First' Council (LSFC) to tackle the problem.

1917 The LSFC's first campaign is to change the pedestrian rule so that walkers face oncoming traffic. Fatal accidents caused by pedestrians stepping into the path of vehicles fall by seventy per cent in the first year.

1918 Establishment of the British Industrial 'Safety First' Association (BISFA).

1923 The National 'Safety First' Association (NSFA) is formed, with both the London 'Safety First' Council and BISFA affiliated to it.

1924 A Safety Code for Road Users is published and half a million copies are distributed – seven years before the Government's first Highway Code is launched.

1933 The government begins to analyse the causes of accidents after pressure from the NSFA.

1941 The NSFA changes its title to the Royal Society for the Prevention of Accidents (RoSPA) with the agreement of King George VI.

1942 RoSPA devises the 'kerb drill' for children.

1945 Work begins with the British Standards Institution to establish safety standards for fireguards.

1947 RoSPA's Cycling Proficiency Scheme begins.

1955 The Finchley League of Safe Drivers is formed by members of Finchley Road Safety Council, becoming the founding organisation of a volunteer network that is subsequently known as RoSPA Advanced Drivers and Riders (RoADAR).

1956 The Sir George Earle Trophy is presented for the first time – RoSPA's premier award for occupational health and safety management.

1958 Cycling Proficiency becomes a national scheme, and more than 100,000 children take part the following year.

1961 The Tufty Club is established, offering road safety training to children, and at its peak there are more than 24,500 registered clubs around the country.

1964 RoSPA begins to campaign for drink-drive legislation, which is subsequently enacted in 1967.

1966 RoSPA celebrates its Golden Jubilee, with the Duke of Edinburgh as its president, and the following year is designated 'Stop Accidents Year' – the charity's biggest ever campaign.

1975 Joint efforts to improve controls on glass installations are made by RoSPA and the Safety Glazing Association, with improved standards subsequently reducing serious injuries from people falling on to glass in the home.

1981 Lord Nugent of Guildford, RoSPA's president, makes a last-minute amendment to the Transport Bill that secures the compulsory wearing of seatbelts in the front of cars, a law that is implemented in 1983.

1987 The campaign for safer foam furnishings begins to bear fruit and, in the years that follow, fire deaths plummet.

1991 After a five-year RoSPA campaign, the government agrees to make it mandatory for domestic appliances to be sold with fitted plugs.

1992 RoSPA marks its seventy-fifth anniversary at London's Guildhall in the presence of HRH The Princess of Wales.

1996 RoSPA publishes its first ideas on the Management of Occupational Road Risk (MORR), being the first organisation to reveal occupational road risk as the 'hidden killer' on Britain's roads.

1998 The LASER – learning about safety by experiencing risk – project is established, through which RoSPA evaluates the growing number of out-of-school safety schemes for children.

1999 Lord Davies of Oldham, RoSPA's deputy president, introduces a Bill in the House of Lords seeking to ban the use of hand-held mobile phones while driving, and a ban is finally achieved in 2003.

2003 The Child Car Seats website, RoSPA's most popular stand-alone website, is launched.

2004 The National Water Safety Forum, co-ordinated by RoSPA, is established, and it goes on to launch WAID – the UK's first national database holding details of all water-related deaths and injuries – in 2009.

2006 RoSPA begins its Injury Database project, to press for the renewed collection of accident causation data through accident and emergency departments.

2009 Safe At Home, England's national home safety equipment scheme, is launched by RoSPA, and it subsequently fits equipment such as fireguards, safety gates and window restrictors in more than 66,000 homes with young children.

2011 RoSPA rediscovers its long-lost archive of vintage safety posters at the back of an old warehouse.

2012 *The Big Book of Accident Prevention* is published by RoSPA, setting out the impact that effective accidental injury prevention can have on public health.

2014 A tougher European standard for internal window blinds is introduced, which is a significant milestone in RoSPA's campaign to stop toddlers being strangled by looped cords.

▶ TIMELINE OF SEATBELT LEGISLATION

1973-74 A clause in the Conservative administration's Road Traffic Bill concerning seat belts was introduced in the Lords. The Bill was dropped.

A similar clause was also included in the subsequent Labour administration's Road Traffic Bill. After a close vote at Report stage in the Lords, the clause was removed. In the new parliament the government introduced it as a separate Bill, but the Second Reading debate was adjourned.

1974-75 After a successful Lords passage, the Bill was adjourned at the Second Reading in the Commons.

1975-76 John Gilbert, Minister of Transport, introduced a Road Traffic (Seat Belts) Bill in February 1976. Later that year, in October, the Bill was due for its final Commons stages. It was withdrawn from business.

1976-77 Two more seat belt Bills were introduced in this session. Both were unsuccessful.

1978-79 In November 1978, Labour MP William Rodgers announced his intention to introduce a seat belts Bill. It completed its First and Second Readings in the House of Commons with a majority of 'almost one hundred'. Labour lost the General Election in 1979 and the Bill was shelved.

1979-80 Neil Carmichael introduced a Private Members' Bill for seat belt compulsion. The proposal was 'talked out' at the Report stage during September 1980.

1980 Lord Nugent of Guildford, RoSPA's president, introduced a Private Members' Bill through the Upper House. It gained a majority of thirty-six at the Second Reading. But, again, the Bill failed.

1981 Lord Nugent seized his chance with an amendment to the Transport Bill. This introduced seat belt wearing for a trial period of three years. RoSPA's president triumphed and the Bill became law... at last.

31 January 1983 The law on compulsory seat belt wearing came into force.

1986 Both Houses of Parliament voted overwhelmingly in favour of retaining the requirement permanently.

1989 Regulations came into effect for mandatory rear seat belt wearing by children.

1991 Wearing a seat belt in the back of a car became compulsory.

Presidents of RoSPA

1917	Lord Sydenham of Combe	1973	Lord Kearton
1919	Viscount Leverhulme	1980	Lord Nugent of Guildford
1923	Lord Armstrong	1982	Earl Cathcart
1925	Viscount Brentford	1986	Lord Brougham and Vaux
1932	Sir Herbert Bain	1989	Lord Keith of Castleacre
1935	Gordon Stewart	1992	Wing Commander G Sinclair
1937	Lord McGowan	1995	Ivan Montgomery
1946	Lord Llewellin	1996	Lord Astor of Hever
1953	Sir Charles Bartlett	1999	Lord Davies of Oldham
1955	Sir Howard Roberts	2001	Lord Faulkner of Worcester
1965	HRH The Prince Philip, Duke of Edinburgh	2004	Baroness Gibson of Market Rasen
1968	Lord Beeching	2008	Lord Jordan of Bournville
		2013	Lord McKenzie of Luton

Bibliography, Sources & Acknowledgements

Beaumont, M and Freeman, M, *The Railway and Modernity*, Peter Lang (Oxford), 2007.

Crary, J, *Suspensions of Perception,* MIT Press (Cambridge, Massachusetts), 2001.

Chambers, E, *Photolitho-offset,* Benn (London), 1967.

Rennie, P, *Modern British Posters*, Black Dog Publishing (London), 2010.

Rennie, P, *RoSPA's Industrial Safety Propaganda during World War II*, UAL London College of Communication PhD thesis (London), 2004.

Raunig, G, *A Thousand Machines,* MIT Press (Cambridge, Massachusetts), 2010.

Saler, M, *The Avant-Garde in Interwar England,* Oxford University Press (Oxford), 1999.

Slocombe, R, *British Posters of World War Two*, Imperial War Museum (London), 2010.

Virilio, P, *Negative Horizon*, Continuum International Publishing (London), 2005.

Weaver, P, *The Technique of Lithography,* Batsford (London), 1964.

ARTICLES: 'England', *Graphis*, Issue 14, 1946.

'British Commercial Art', *Graphis*, Issue 31, 1950, p.206.

'Warning Signs English Prevention of Accidents Posters', *Gebrauchsgraphik*, Issue 2, Feb 1950, p.33.

ACKNOWLEDGEMENTS

There are a number of people whose support has facilitated this project and who deserve thanks. Tom Mullarkey, the Chief Executive of RoSPA, and his colleagues, Janice Cave and Jo Bullock, rediscovered the poster archive and recognised its significance. Without their support, this book would not have been possible.

I would also like to thank my academic colleagues who supported this project in its earliest form, especially Janice Hart and Jeremy Aynsley, who supervised my original research. Finally, thanks to all individuals who have helped and supported my work on the RoSPA poster archive.

ILLUSTRATION CREDITS

All posters reproduced in this book are from RoSPA's archive or the Author's Collection, except pages 90 and 92–94, courtesy, Library of Congress. The posters on pages 18 and 115 by Abram Games are copyright © Estate of Abram Games and are reproduced here by their kind permission.